GARDENWALKS SERIES

GARDENWALKS

IN THE PACIFIC NORTHWEST

*Beautiful Gardens along the Coast
from Oregon to British Columbia*

ALICE JOYCE

INSIDERS' GUIDE®

GUILFORD, CONNECTICUT
AN IMPRINT OF THE GLOBE PEQUOT PRESS

The prices, rates, and hours listed in this guidebook were confirmed at press time. We recommend, however, that you call establishments to obtain current information before traveling.

INSIDERS' GUIDE ®

Cover photo of Washington Park's Japanese Garden (Portland, OR)
Text design by Diane Gleba Hall
Illustrations by Ted Enik and Carole Drong
Maps by Mary Ballachino © Morris Book Publishing, LLC

Joyce, Alice, 1946–
    Gardenwalks in the Pacific Northwest : beautiful gardens along the Coast from Oregon to British Columbia / Alice Joyce.—1st ed.
        p. cm. — (Gardenwalks series)
    Includes index.
    ISBN 0-7627-3818-9
    1. Gardens—Northwest, Pacific—Guidebooks. 2. Northwest, Pacific—Guidebooks. I. Title. II. Series.

SB466.U65N76 2006
712.09795—dc22   2005055248

Manufactured in the United States of America
First Edition/First Printing

Contents

Gardenwalks in Oregon

Acknowledgments

Writing my first book, *West Coast Gardenwalks*, opened up a world of change. Even before the book was published, my husband, Tom, and I embarked on a head-spinning move cross-country. I began planting a garden from scratch during the El Niño rains of 1998–99 while completing the book's final rewrite from our new home in Northern California.

In teaming up with The Globe Pequot Press for *Gardenwalks in the Pacific Northwest*, I have greatly expanded on the original material. Each region is now covered in-depth and includes wonderful gardens that have recently appeared on the horticultural landscape.

There is so much to learn from each of the gardens I visit, or revisit. It gives me great pleasure to reconnect with gardening cohorts, and it's equally gratifying to forge new associations.

I regret not being able to list everyone by name, but I sincerely thank the horticulturists and designers, garden directors, and dedicated staff who have shared their enthusiasm and love of plants with me. Thank you for bringing to light all aspects of making a garden and for taking time to assist my efforts to provide accurate information.

Introduction

$\mathcal{G}$ARDENWALKS *in the Pacific Northwest* takes its cue from *West Coast Gardenwalks,* a guidebook that came about as a result of my quest to discover gardens where plants reign and the art of garden design flourishes. Public landscapes, private retreats, commercial nurseries, suppliers of garden-oriented paraphernalia—all interested me as I became ever more enthusiastic (actually, quite dotty) about cultivating the tiny parcel of urban property to the front and rear of my former home in Chicago.

My husband, Tom, and I were lured by the sensory pleasures of beautiful gardens. Our all-too-brief vacations revolved more and more around visits to botanical gardens and arboretums, to specialty growers of rare plants, and to well-stocked shops purveying fine garden tools, supplies, and unusual products for gardening buffs.

We spent countless hours in used bookstores, where I perused musty old garden tomes and botanical illustrations. Tom, a patient man who enjoys bird-watching and revels in examining the myriad insects one encounters in garden settings, generally stalked different aisles, examining antiquated medical books or field guides listing the exotic fauna of whatever region we happened to be visiting.

But before embarking on each of our journeys, I would commence my search for a guidebook—one that would contain a wealth of information on an extensive range of garden locales, together with notable resources of particular appeal to someone like myself who suffers quite contentedly from gardening fever.

Since I could never find the type of gardener's travel guide I was looking for, I decided to write one myself.

I couldn't know at the time that the project would open doors to a life I could only have imagined.

Today I enjoy tending a lush sanctuary surrounding our home in Marin County: a year-round habitat garden enlivened by bees, butterflies, and the incessant whir of hummingbirds feasting on the vivid blooms of salvias, cupheas, and *Phygelius*.

The Garden Walks features I write for the *San Francisco Chronicle* propel me to seek out gardens near and far, and I continue to discover convivial landscapes in the United States and points beyond. Recent travels to explore gardens in France and England have reinforced my appreciation of and appetite for the diverse gardenscapes of North America's West Coast.

A note about specialty nurseries: Garden travelers might be overwhelmed by the multitude of nurseries encountered while exploring the Pacific Northwest. Rather than attempt to provide a comprehensive listing, I've included in the gardenwalks write-ups a sampling of nurseries. Many carry distinctive plant genera or unusual selections. Looking for a rare native species? Perhaps you're in pursuit of clematis or uncommon tropicals. Be sure to visit these exciting enterprises located within easy driving distance of major cities or in close proximity to highways.

I encourage you to find opportunities to talk with the spirited entrepreneurs responsible for overseeing day-to-day nursery operations. During my travels, chatting about plants never fails to prove enlightening. You, too, can take advantage of such occasions to learn as much as possible about unfamiliar varieties that will frequently be a cut above ordinary nursery stock. It's inspirational to meet dedicated horticulturists who earn their living promoting the plants they most cherish. These conversations might foster new ways of thinking about gardening, setting into motion ideas for renewing or revamping the plantings in your own garden back home.

All the information in these pages has been carefully checked, but please note that a garden's open hours, admission fees, etc., are always subject to change. In the case of bed-and-breakfast inns and garden-oriented businesses, ownership can change along with pricing, types of accommodations, and particular offerings. So whether planning a short jaunt or lengthy vacation, phone first before setting out to assure your sojourn is a pleasant one.

Of course, the qualities I find most alluring about a given garden setting may not necessarily delight every garden traveler. Still, I trust that the material compiled here will provide guidance in choosing places that will appeal to your own inclinations.

If you do not find an entry you are looking for, it may be because I am asked at times to exclude a garden if its residential location places limits on public visitation. In general, my travels follow a more-or-less coastal orientation, and I do not attempt to cover the entire landscape of a state.

I'd like to hear about your garden adventures: the high points, as well as any plans that may not have turned out as expected. Send an e-mail to westcoastgrdnwalks@yahoo.com, or write to me c/o The Globe Pequot Press, P.O. Box 480, Guilford, CT 06437-0480. Let me know what gardens or activities you found most appealing. From one garden lover to another, here's wishing you the best of times on your gardenwalks!

How to Use This Book

$\mathcal{P}$ERUSE the garden entries in this book and you'll find major public gardens along with private dominions and specialty plant nurseries. I've included a chapter called "Thoughts on Garden Styles," which gives an overview of what you may see in the Pacific Northwest; a chapter on garden lodgings; an idiosyncratic selection of resources for gardeners; and a glossary of garden terms.

The chapters of this book are organized roughly from north to south, following the coast from British Columbia to Oregon. Within each chapter, gardenwalks are organized alphabetically by town. Details about admission fees, open hours, tours, and driving directions are placed immediately following the garden descriptions. You'll also find information on wheelchair accessibility.

The garden numbers correspond to the numbers on the maps at the beginning of each chapter. Consult the maps to plan an itinerary of garden visits, or choose gardens with a specific theme by referring to the "Choosing an Outing" chapter, or pick a garden simply by the appeal of its features!

You'll find sidebars throughout the chapters. They point out nearby places of interest, highlight remarkable garden tours and shows, or reveal special things to look for during a garden visit.

Keep in mind that it's important to call ahead to confirm hours and to obtain detailed directions. In many cases, gardens or plant nurseries are open to the public on designated days or by appointment only. Business hours may be limited during winter, or a garden or nursery may be closed for the season. A few minutes of extra planning will make your gardenwalk explorations that much more rewarding.

Thoughts on Garden Styles

OFTEN I'M ASKED to name my favorite garden or coaxed to reveal the type of garden I prefer. In truth, I embrace the exceptional variety of garden sanctuaries and encompassing landscapes I have come to know, because each in its own way stimulates my imagination and wakens my senses. Here are some of the garden styles you'll come across on your Pacific Northwest gardenwalks.

ARBORETUMS
ARBORETUMS are peaceful places where the mind is soothed. Wander through copses of old-growth trees and you appreciate simple pleasures, like observing the light that filters through the leaves. Deciduous trees manifest seasonal shifts, putting us directly in touch with eternal cycles of the natural world. Throughout the year, we are rewarded as trees leaf out, display autumn color, or signal the advent of winter with the rustle of fallen leaves underfoot. Even

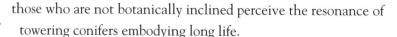

those who are not botanically inclined perceive the resonance of towering conifers embodying long life.

Yet one powerful storm can wreak havoc, felling countless trees and understory plantings. Mature trees, too, eventually meet their end. A course of maintenance is continuous, requiring ailing specimens to be removed and new trees to be planted.

Arboretums recognize the public's need for natural areas. As stewards, arboretums perpetuate and preserve essential forested spaces, cultivating a wealth of tree species that enhance our lives. When escape from the city is not possible, we find in these leafy preserves a respite from street noise and the drone of traffic.

BOTANICAL GARDENS

A UNIQUE STATE of awareness unfolds once we set about exploring the realms of a botanical garden. Here we enter a gateway that brings us in touch with cultivated flora from the far corners of the earth.

The botanical garden is a place of beauty and learning that allows us to become familiar with unusual, eye-catching species, labeled to help identify the plants. Educational signage further guides us, providing lessons in geography and giving relevant details about botanical families and relationships between plants.

Coherent communities of plants are set out to provide maximum interest and impact, so that we might wander from a lavish bed overflowing with summery displays of dahlias to a glade of graceful maple trees to artfully arranged acres of alpine specimens.

The range of plants is as wide as the distance between continents. Naturalistic alliances of flora extend over rolling terrain open to the sky or enliven shady paths running through a intricate sequence of blossoming shrubs.

Native plant displays enlighten garden visitors and conservation-minded green thumbs alike. On-site sales are the special province of garden propagators and volunteers, who encourage home gardeners to acquire native shrubs, perennials, a young sapling, or rare ephemeral woodland bulbs. Oftentimes these species are perfectly suited to the conditions in our own backyards, resulting in naturalized plantings that carry on the garden's message.

CONSERVATORY GARDENS

IN MARKED CONTRAST, we are transported to another realm entirely when in the presence of exotic plants grown sequestered within a conservatory or glasshouse.

Conservatory exhibitions provide complete sensory experiences, luring us along corridors dense with moisture and laden with fragrance. Extravagant floral displays offer a thrilling break from reality, especially when the atmosphere outdoors is bleak or cold. A stroll beneath tropical palm trees sets the stage for a languid interlude from everyday cares.

Observing plant life in the discrete space of a beautifully constructed glasshouse, we depart from all that is familiar when we come upon species threatened in the wild: Groupings of cycads, for example, rivet our attention, with their expressive bearing and eye-catching cones.

Seize the chance to immerse yourself in arrays of flora exemplified by lush, oversize foliage, bizarre plant forms, even malodorous blooms appealing to flies alone, and discover a milieu that exists beyond the borders of your own hometown.

SUCCULENT GARDENS

PRICKLY CACTI, epiphytes that draw nourishment from the air, and other tender succulents often make up conservatory displays, where the staggering scope of plant architecture is a design lesson to be gleaned. The greenery we normally encounter in a garden is not present. Instead, we encounter an assertive aloe armed with red teeth playing off a rotund cactus, or the sharp-tipped, lancelike leaves of yuccas set off by the blushed-mauve, fleshy foliage of echeverias.

At the conservatory in Seattle's Volunteer Park, visitors are transported to an otherworldly atmosphere. Discover the Cactus House landscape populated by thorny euphorbias and columnar cacti armed with provocative spines, and it is suddenly possible to imagine ourselves far away in Madagascar or South Africa.

Artistry and gardening prowess come together in a succulent garden's sculptural installation of living plant material. Succulents

also give rise to splendid exhibitions of flowers. Altogether unexpected is the sight of these odd prickly plants aglow with tubular flowers in fiery tones of coral, tangerine, and lemon yellow.

PACIFIC NORTHWEST STYLE

THE PRESERVATION of estates like the Butchart Gardens allows us to experience a refined atmosphere associated with gardens and eras long past. We recognize links between contemporary garden design and the rich history and art of Italian and French landscape traditions—and furthermore, we appreciate a distinctive Pacific Northwest style.

The Butchart Gardens' Italian Garden makes reference to the idealized gardens of the Renaissance, from lovely hardscaping and sculptural ornamentation to the harmonious symmetry of a formal pool. Yet a verdant backdrop of broadleaf evergreens and majestic conifers enlarges in essential ways upon the grandeur of the landscaping.

In the Northwest, lavish emerald greenery associates assuredly with seasonal flowering displays in gardenscapes that are often set apart by great natural beauty. Perched high above the Willamette River, Elk Rock, the Garden at the Bishop's Close, offers affecting vistas of Mount Hood. Other emotions come into play, too, as we pass from one garden room to the next hidden space. Enjoying a palpable sense of mystery, we wonder what horticultural delight or surprising view awaits around the next corner.

A place of unparalleled aesthetic enjoyment, the Bloedel Reserve displays a sensitive melding of cultivated layouts, an encompassing forest, and a sweeping scene of Puget Sound. Ephemeral trilliums bloom in the Glen area, their lyric springtime display illustrating the kind of year-round magic to be found along each hushed, ribboned pathway through the reserve's property.

Exemplifying Northwest style, the Bloedel Reserve reveals an overall composition of restorative clarity in the modern, geometric outline of the Reflection Pool and in the contemplative Japanese Garden, especially when lit by fall color. Welcoming meadow, marsh, and woodland habitats all are at one within the cool green, pristine landscape.

A more recent setting serves to advance the notion of Pacific Northwest style: Created by Daniel Hinkley and Robert Jones, the gardens at Heronswood Nursery feature a framework of atmospheric water features, graceful walkways, inventive topiary hedging, and sumptuous medleys of plants nestled in a classic Northwest setting of towering Douglas firs.

A renowned author, lecturer, and plant explorer, Hinkley stirs up the gardening milieu by fashioning Heronswood's garden spaces into a haven for exhilarating rarities and memorable varieties. Gardeners subjected to plant lust are enthralled by the utterly distinctive descriptions Hinkley penned for years in the nursery's annual catalog. Likewise, the Heronswood landscape entices an international gaggle of garden lovers wishing to experience a modern-day kingdom of plants.

ASIAN GARDENS

THOUSANDS OF YEARS of garden making and plant cultivation contribute to the recorded history of Chinese gardens.

A governing principle is man's oneness with the universe. And while it would be possible to write a treatise on symbolism in the Chinese garden, it is significant, nonetheless, to note the potent imagery and imposing character of specific components: Ancient tree stumps function as monuments. Mountainous reconstructions of rockwork serve to imitate or recapture natural scenery. Distinctive specimen rocks command our attention as individual sculptures,

each possessing its own illusive features. The rustic qualities of stone stairways join garden space to rural setting.

Architecturally the Chinese garden is stunning. Its pavilions and pagodas are surrounded by lakes. Colonnades and temple buildings are set within courtyards. All stand out due to finely crafted embellishments. Wood carvings and clay roof tiles appear, as do vibrant paint color and applications of gilt. Ornamental pathways are paved skillfully with small stones, rendered to evoke waves or peacock feathers. Walls that sequester the buildings display the myriad shapes of windows and doors, outlining entrances to the hallowed space or luring one to gaze upon a particular framed view.

A venerable tree is always accorded honor and treated as a centerpiece, while flowering displays are conspicuous for their naturalism. Rather than placed in orderly, contained plantings, the magnolias, azaleas and rhododendrons, tree peonies, cherries, and camellias are sited in a manner that appears spontaneous.

In the Japanese garden, subtlety and an essential tranquillity are keynotes. The garden is a sacred realm. The design tradition looks to the natural world for inspiration, and within the design aesthetic, interpretation comes into play through symbolic elements revolving around the representation of mountains, sea and islands, forests, and streams.

The hand of the designer shapes the space to reflect philosophical and religious constructs, thereby setting the stage for a meditative experience.

Zen Buddhist gardens incorporate arrangements of rocks and raked gravel to refer to mountain vistas, waterfalls, and rivers. Elements may allude to multilayered allegories as a way of imparting Zen fundamentals. The Japanese tea garden is a place of spiritual passage, exemplifying beliefs associated with tea ceremony.

Spacious stroll gardens are idealized landscapes, where a lofty artistry is achieved over time. All the senses are engaged as we experience evanescent blooms, the careful shaping of plant specimens, mossy expanses, and handmade fences, all ushering in lovely aspects of color, form, and spatial harmony. To punctuate the space, sculpted

stone water basins and lanterns appear. Precarious stepping-stones and arching bridges draw us to explore the meandering shape of a pond with vivid koi and, farther forward, the evocative scenery.

MODERNIST GARDENS

MODERNIST GARDENS redefine traditional approaches to designing space: Simplicity is a powerful influence. Environmental issues or ecological concerns may come into play, or metaphor and allusion may prevail.

Is it a garden if there are no plants? The visions of talented landscape architects and designers are made manifest through innovative materials used in startling ways. Artificial devices may demand that we recognize a different paradigm: Can bright plastic elements be a substitute for greenery?

Conceptual underpinnings challenge our basic assumptions about the nature/notion of a garden, so that we are required to contemplate individual interpretations of the garden theme. The contemporary designer who creates an innovative twenty-first-century garden envisions concepts that go beyond the traditional, bridging the realm of environmental artists.

Gardenwalks in British Columbia

Vancouver and Vicinity
Gardenwalks

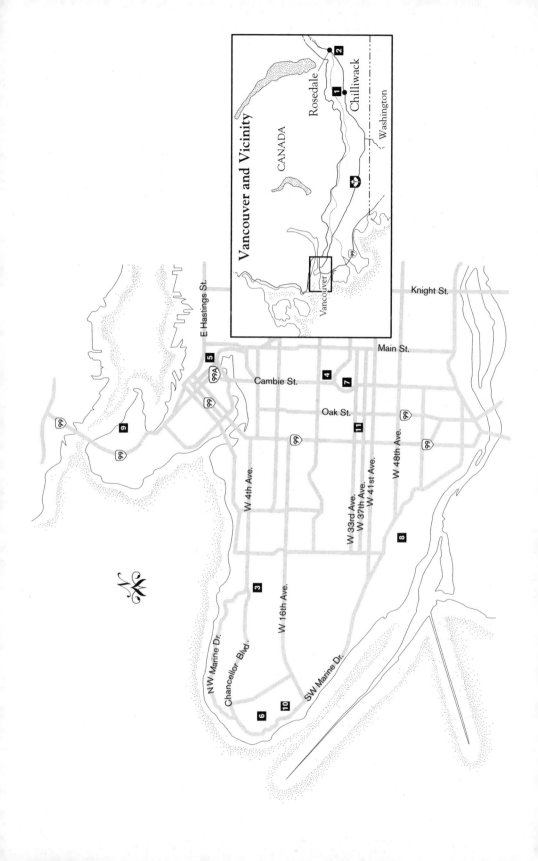

Vancouver and Vicinity

CANADA

Rosedale

Chilliwack

Washington

Vancouver

Knight St.

E Hastings St.

Main St.

99A

Cambie St.

99

Oak St.

99

99

9

99

W 4th Ave.

W 33rd Ave.

W 37th Ave.

W 41st Ave.

W 48th Ave.

W 16th Ave.

NW Marine Dr.

Chancellor Blvd.

SW Marine Dr.

1. Chilliwack: Minter Country Garden Centre
2. Rosedale: Minter Gardens
3. Vancouver: Arthur Erickson House and Garden
4. Vancouver: Bloedel Floral Conservatory at Queen Elizabeth Park
5. Vancouver: Dr. Sun Yat-Sen Classical Chinese Garden
6. Vancouver: Nitobe Memorial Garden
7. Vancouver: Queen Elizabeth Park
8. Vancouver: Southlands Nursery Ltd.
9. Vancouver: Stanley Park
10. Vancouver: University of British Columbia Botanical Garden
11. Vancouver: VanDusen Botanical Garden

1. Minter Country Garden Centre

10015 Young Road North, **Chilliwack,** BC V2P 4V4;
(604) 792–6612, (800) 661–3919; www.mintergardens.com

THE EIGHTEEN-ACRE Minter Country Garden Centre is situated in Chilliwack, twelve minutes west of Minter Gardens. Along with a lively schedule of demonstrations and classes ranging from composting to holiday decorating to historical workshops, the center offers greenhouses, florists, and a wealth of uncommon plants for sale that will pique the interest of both budding and knowledgeable gardeners.

A passenger train provides rides around the plant nursery and through the adjacent nature preserve, where you'll discover a large pond that serves as a bird sanctuary. In the midst of the preserve, a suspension bridge highlights a water garden. Depending on the season, there are colorful garden displays. Children can visit bunnies and emu, so there's something to entertain young and old alike.

Admission: Free; fee for train ride.

Garden open: Year-round. Hours of operation vary; call for details. Closed December 25 and 26, and January 1 and 2.

Further information: The Callicarpa Garden Café offers freshly baked treats and lunches daily; call for details. From mid-September to June, the Wine Store features 300 wines from British Columbia; in summer the store is open at Minter Gardens. The center is mostly wheelchair accessible.

Directions: Located approximately ninety minutes east of the city of Vancouver, the center is near downtown Chilliwack. Take exit 119 westbound or exit 120 eastbound on Trans-Canada Highway 1.

2. Minter Gardens

52892 Bunker Road, **Rosedale,** BC (Mailing address: P.O. Box 40,
Chilliwack, BC V2P 6H7); (604) 794–7191 (April to October),
(604) 792–3799 (November to March), (888) 646–8377;
www.mintergardens.com

*M*AJESTIC mountains provide a stunning backdrop to the
Minter Gardens landscape. Rising 7,000 feet, Mount
Cheam displays its snowcapped form from mid-September until the
brilliant summer sun melts away its frosted mantle. Totaling thirty-
two acres, Minter Gardens presents visitors with flamboyant arrays
of flowers and exuberant greenery in the form of emerald-colored
lawns balanced by stately mature trees. Its design will delight adults
and children alike.

These gardens began taking shape in 1978 when Brian and
Faye Minter purchased the property after being captivated by the
site's beauty. Its fascinating topography is the result of an ancient
mountain slide. The gardens were established with rustic buildings
designed by architect Peter Thornton. Rock retaining walls made
use of the beautiful hard shale found on the land. They exhibit the
craftsmanship of Kevan Maxwell, a local landscaper and stonemason. Finally, water was discovered after drilling hundreds of feet
into the earth, providing a source for the gardens' streams, fountains,
and small lakes.

Fun Features for Children

Minter Gardens in Rosedale captures the fancy of children as well
as adults. The young (and the young at heart) will enjoy the
largest floral flag in Canada, floral topiaries, and a flower bed that
spells out the Minter Gardens name. Another floral display
includes the merry figures of Snow White and the Seven Dwarfs!

You'll find eleven different theme gardens at Minter Gardens, a very family-friendly spot. Explore the gardens' Nature Trail, Aviaries, and Vintage Waterwheel and Mill Pond. One of the more compelling displays, the Evergreen Maze, presents its inviting challenge to all who pass by.

Framed by a regal archway, springtime displays of tulips and flowering cherry trees precede summer's blooms in the Rose Garden. An ample courtyard also features a display of bulbs to herald each new gardening year. Not long thereafter azaleas, dogwoods, magnolias, and fine displays of "rhodies," of course, illuminate the Rhododendron Garden.

Lavish annuals abound during the warm summer months, with colorful begonias performing unceasingly before a waterfall that seems to proclaim the passage of melting snows from the surrounding mountains. Dahlias strut their stuff in September, along with heaps of fall crocuses (*Colchicum*). Once in full swing, an autumn spectacle is presided over by brilliant maples looking down over beds filled with specimens such as cool-hued flowering kale and cabbage, chrysanthemums, and pansies. There's still more to see here, especially the recent addition of two new Victorian-style conservatories: Envision Garden Conservatory and Trillium Restaurant Conservatory.

❀ **Admission:** Fee.

Garden open: Daily. April and October: 10:00 A.M. to 5:00 P.M. May and September: 9:00 A.M. to 5:30 P.M. June: 9:00 A.M. to 6:00 P.M. July and August: 9:00 A.M. to 7:00 P.M. Gardens may close early due to inclement weather.

Further information: Enjoy a lunch buffet at the Trillium Restaurant Conservatory: Call (604) 794–7044 or the toll free number listed above. Enjoy casual dining in the Envision Conservatory Garden Cafe; phone for hours. Horticultural and general guided tours are available for a fee but must be booked in advance. Check the Web site for a calendar of special events. The Minter Country Wines shop offers complimentary daily wine tasting in the summer months; phone (604) 794–5888 for hours. Minter Gardens is wheelchair accessible.

Directions: Minter Gardens is located approximately ninety minutes east of the city of Vancouver or three hours from Victoria, Vancouver Island. To reach Minter Gardens, take exit 135 off Trans-Canada 1 and follow signs.

3. Arthur Erickson House and Garden

P.O. Box 39042, **Vancouver,** BC V6R 4P1; (604) 738–4195; www.arthurerickson.com

*A*N ESTEEMED architect known for his design of the Museum of Anthropology at the University of British Columbia and for other such stunning buildings, Vancouver-born Arthur Erickson shaped the two city lots surrounding his home into a fascinating and unique garden setting.

Listed on the Vancouver Heritage Register, the Arthur Erickson House and Garden hint of a wild, verdant place, yet Erickson's most personal creation embodies a singular modernism influenced by West Coast and Japanese garden style.

Soon after purchasing the parcel in 1957, Erickson edited out the existing cottage-style English garden. In a stroke of genius, he created a high berm to shield the space from the house across the way. A pond was Erickson's answer to the spot where the earth had been removed.

Today the garden's lush vegetation includes flourishing arrays of native plants and gracefully arching groves of bamboo, effectively complementing the water feature.

Dense plantings blanket the fence around the property, cocooning the space in its own serenely composed environment. Look for Erickson's masterful touch as it's revealed in the garden's disparate elements. The exacting placement of a stone slab, for instance, constitutes a moon-viewing platform that appears to float atop the pond.

For a stimulating and enchanting sojourn, plan a visit to the Arthur Erickson House and Garden.

❀ **Admission:** Fee.

Garden open: Year-round by appointment only.

Further information: Call to book a tour with the Arthur Erickson House and Garden Foundation. The garden may be visited in conjunction with the Garden Conservancy's Open Days Program; see listing in the resources chapter. Wheelchair accessibility is limited.

Directions: The garden is in Vancouver's West Point Grey area. Address and directions are provided when an appointment is confirmed.

4. Bloedel Floral Conservatory at Queen Elizabeth Park

Thirty-third Avenue at Cambie Street, **Vancouver,** BC; (604) 257–8584

*S*HOULD YOU happen upon rain while visiting Vancouver (but regardless of the weather forecast!), make it a point to seek out the Bloedel Conservatory. You'll encounter a tantalizing, sultry environment within the conservatory's tropical microclimate. North America's second-largest single-structure conservatory, Bloedel opened to the public in 1969. At present, the conservatory exhibits more than 500 species of plants from the rain forest, the subtropics, and the desert.

Beneath the conservatory's impressive geodesic dome, iridescent parrots and free-flying tropical birds find shelter. These beautiful creatures count among a host of some one hundred types of engagingly vocal birds inhabiting the conservatory's magnificent floral jungle. Tantalizing water gardens compel visitors' eyes back to earth, where sleek koi fish swim contentedly amid continuous exhibitions of fragrant blooms.

Perched atop Queen Elizabeth Park, Bloedel Conservatory will charm you with its collections of extravagant flora and exotic birds.

❀ **Admission:** Fee.

Garden open: Daily; hours vary throughout the year. Call for details. Closed December 25. The gift shop is open during regular hours.

Further information: The gift shop carries souvenirs and novelty items. Seasons in the Park restaurant is located only 150 meters (500 feet) away from the conservatory; see the Queen Elizabeth Park entry for details. The conservatory and gift shop are fully wheelchair accessible.

Directions: The conservatory is located at the top of Queen Elizabeth Park; see directions in the entry for the park.

5. Dr. Sun Yat-Sen Classical Chinese Garden

578 Carrall Street, **Vancouver,** BC V6B 5K2; (604) 662–3207; www.vancouverchinesegarden.com

*E*ACH ELEMENT in the classical Chinese garden speaks symbolically of human values and philosophical truths. In the context of such a garden, the precise placement of a delicate plant or formidable boulder carries with it layers of meaning. Modeled after the private gardens of the Ming dynasty (1368–1644), Vancouver's remarkable Dr. Sun Yat-Sen Classical Chinese Garden is believed to be the first authentic full-size garden of its kind ever constructed outside China. The garden opened to the public in April 1986.

Taoism in the Garden

The Dr. Sun Yat-Sen Garden in Vancouver—like all classical Chinese gardens—demonstrates the Taoist principles of yin and yan. To understand the garden's enclosed environment is to appreciate a balance between contrasting forces: A motionless pool of water is reflective of yin; a craggy pine grasping a rock's surface illustrates yang. Observe softness, and you'll note an opposing hard density, and so on. This garden can change the way you look at the world around you.

Funding for the garden came about through the combined efforts of three branches of government in Canada, the People's Republic of China, and private donors. The building of the Dr. Sun Yat-Sen Classical Chinese Garden was a major project that called upon the expertise of local designers working closely with a large team of accomplished artisans from Suzhou, China's Garden City. Now garden lovers need only to travel to Chinatown in Vancouver to have the unique opportunity of visiting a classical Chinese garden.

The classical Chinese garden traditionally incorporates four primary elements: buildings, rocks, plants, and water. At the Dr. Sun Yat-Sen Garden, you'll glimpse venerable Tai Hu limestone rocks, their jagged forms connoting the essence of a rough landscape. Oftentimes a rock stands as a sculptural monolith. High walls define the garden's overall space and make reference to the cosmos itself, with windows opening to embrace surprising views beyond.

The different flora of this Chinese garden symbolizes a range of human virtues. The garden's *Plant Guide* makes clear how the plum blossom, for instance, embodies the idea of rebirth, while winter-blooming chrysanthemums are representative of courage. Alluring magnolia trees, spirited climbing hydrangeas, and magnificent tree peonies bearing lavish multipetaled flowers offer their radiant beauty to replenish one's soul. In studying the garden's plants, we are led to examine the deeper implications of carefully arranged pine and bamboo, weeping willow and ginkgo. Once we have gained an understanding of the precepts of the classical Chinese garden, we become increasingly able to decipher the symbolism of the garden and recognize illustrations of such traits as strength and resiliency, grace and courage, a nourished spirit, and a developed mind.

Visit the Dr. Sun Yat-Sen Garden for a unique cultural encounter. Admire the classical Chinese architecture with its beautiful lattice woodwork; finely crafted, hand-fired roof tiles; and patterned hardscaping composed of cool-hued stones. Notice how the repetition of geometric shapes in the stone creates motifs that contribute to the serenity of the setting. Observe the ways in which the garden's aesthetic sensibilities differ from the preconceived norms of Western landscape design, and you'll appreciate the garden's luminous atmosphere. It expresses a philosophy that remains as vibrant today as it was hundreds of years ago in a faraway setting.

❀ **Admission:** Fee.

Garden open: Year-round. Phone for hours.

Further information: Guided tours depart at regular intervals throughout the day and are included in the admission fee; call or check the Web site for tour times. Visit the Web site for a list of special events and public programs. The gift shop features interesting and lovely items. Wheelchair accessibility is limited.

Directions: The garden is a few minutes east of downtown in Vancouver's Chinatown neighborhood, on the corner of Carrall Street and Keefer Street. Columbia Street runs along the garden's eastern boundary, while Pender Street runs along the northern boundary, leading up in the direction of Stanley Park.

6. Nitobe Memorial Garden

1903 West Mall, **Vancouver,** BC V6T 1Z2; (604) 822–6038 (gatehouse), (604) 822–9666; www.nitobe.org

*A*CKNOWLEDGED to be one of the finest classical Japanese gardens outside Japan, Nitobe Memorial Garden honors Dr. Inazo Nitobe, a scholar and diplomat who worked to foster a bridge between nations. Highly regarded in the art of garden design, landscape architect Professor Kannosuke Mori of Japan both designed and supervised the actual building of Nitobe Memorial Garden.

In the spring Nitobe Memorial Garden is aglow with the blossoms of flowering cherry trees brought from Japan to be installed in this serene Vancouver setting. A tranquil spell is cast on all who walk the garden's impeccably groomed paths, with native trees and shrubs growing among thriving azaleas, Japanese irises, and a gathering of maples especially imported from Japan.

Overall, the style of Nitobe Memorial Garden is informal. The Strolling Garden beckons visitors across the portal of its ceremonial gateway. Placed along walkways are perfectly situated benches, together with six distinctive bridges made of wood and stone, aimed at directing wanderers to admire the garden's fertile landscape and aesthetically pleasing views.

The garden's waterfalls, with their pacifying sounds, encourage contemplation and invite repose. Suggesting nature's perfection is

an essential part of the artistry of a Japanese garden. Here such elements as an artificial "mountain," an island, and a lake complete this artistic feat.

Stone lanterns ornament the garden. Uniquely designed and of subtle beauty, these lanterns accentuate the forms of plants and their myriad shades of foliage, from deep jade to bright chartreuse. Seasonally, the setting's monochromatic plantings enjoy infusions of color. In spring cherry blossoms and azaleas enliven the scenery with their pleasing palette of many hues, while beautiful blue irises lend cool accents to summer scenes. Sumptuous scarlets and the tawny color of tangerines appear as Japanese maples turn color in fall.

In Japanese culture, tea ceremony and garden art are closely linked. At Nitobe Memorial Garden you'll find an exquisite Teahouse Rock Garden, with paths of crushed rock surrounding a characteristic teahouse, fabricated of Hinoki cypress. The tea ceremony still takes place, at times, in this lovely building.

A Vancouver sojourn would be incomplete without a visit to this exceptional, authentically designed Japanese garden.

❀ **Admission:** Fee.

Garden open: Daily 10:00 A.M. to 6:00 P.M. in summer; call ahead or check the Web site for dates and hours during other seasons.

Further information: There are no food or restroom facilities at the garden. A double entry ticket may be purchased for the University of British Columbia Botanical Garden and Nitobe Memorial Garden. Nitobe's paths are not paved.

Directions: Nitobe Memorial Garden is on Northwest Marine Drive, 3 kilometers (nearly 2 miles) north of the botanical garden. A map of the UBC campus can be downloaded from the Web site. (See the UBC Botanical Garden entry for further information.)

7. Queen Elizabeth Park

Twenty-ninth Street to Thirty-seventh Street and Cambie Street
to Ontario Street, **Vancouver,** BC (park district mailing address:
30 East Thirtieth Avenue, Vancouver, BC V5V 2T9);
(604) 257–8400 (Vancouver Board of Parks and Recreation);
www.city.vancouver.bc.ca/parks

*C*ONVENIENTLY located in central Vancouver, Queen Elizabeth
Park attracts millions of visitors each year who look forward
to enjoying the park's immaculately maintained grounds, excellent
arboretum, sunken quarry gardens, and ever-popular Bloedel Floral
Conservatory.

Encompassing 130 acres, Queen Elizabeth Park inhabits a
lovely city garden setting and features rolling hillsides planted with
a remarkable variety of Canada's native trees and exotic species.
Referred to by residents as Little Mountain, the 500-foot elevation
at the park's summit is the highest point within the city of Vancouver, affording an encompassing 360-degree view of the downtown
skyline and mountain backdrop.

In the spring Queen Elizabeth Park is a wonderland of flowering trees and shrubs. This season also yields a tapestry of radiant
bulbs that illuminates the encircling greenery. Parading annuals are
installed once summer arrives, affording colorful tableaux that enliven the park during those months when many travelers are drawn
to Vancouver's picturesque gardens.

In 1969 the Bloedel Conservatory geodesic dome was constructed, adding another not-to-be-missed feature to this exceptional parkland. Look for a powerful sculpture by Henry Moore
arising on the plaza east of the conservatory.

Walk around the north and northwest sections skirting the
park and you'll discover the park's arboretum plantings, which feature native as well as exotic trees.

You'll also find a small garden of roses being developed on the southwestern edge of the park.

❁ **Admission:** Free.

Garden open: Daily, dawn to dusk.

Further information: Enjoy brunch, lunch, or a great dinner—along with an unparalleled view of Vancouver—from the glass-enclosed Seasons in the Park Restaurant; phone (800) 632–9422 or (604) 874–8008 for reservations. The restaurant's hours can be found at www.vancouverdine.com. Parking is available along Queen Elizabeth Park Drive and in the parking lot west of Bloedel Conservatory near the Thirty-third Avenue and Cambie Street entrance to the park. You'll find a detailed map of the park on the Web site, with information on horticultural features, customer services, and wheelchair-accessible areas such as pathways, sidewalks, and facilities. Wheelchair routes are marked on the pavement in the large Quarry Garden and Lookout Plaza; however, many areas (including the Rose Garden and much of the arboretum) are not fully accessible.

Directions: Queen Elizabeth Park is ten minutes south of the downtown area, about 1 mile east of Granville Street; ½ mile east of Oak Street (Highway 99).

8. Southlands Nursery Ltd.

6550 Balaclava Street, **Vancouver,** BC V6N 1L9; (604) 261–6411

*I*N AN UPSCALE Vancouver neighborhood, an equestrian area near the University of British Columbia Botanical Garden, is a very special nursery. You will want to schedule a foray to plantsman extraordinaire Tom Hobbs's Southlands Nursery.

Reigning over Vancouver's "hort" scene, Hobbs appears on television and presents rousing lectures on garden design across the country. He has created a glorious private garden that attests to his talent and creativity.

"Beauty before profit" is Hobbs's motto for the nursery, where stunning plant combinations displayed in picture-perfect vignettes await. You simply must see the inventive ways in which texture, form, and flower are melded here. A New Zealand sedge, for example, provides an agreeable aspect of verticality at the top of a hanging arrangement that overflows with the vivid blooms and heart-shaped leaves of *Rhodochiton atrosanguineum*; the succulent "string of pearls" rains down to form a beaded edging.

Equally as effective, the same string of pearls (*Senecio rowleyanus*) plant cascades from the top of a terra-cotta statue of a mythical youth balancing a basket on his head. The simplicity of the planting is beguiling.

Dip into Hobbs's book, *The Jewel Box Garden* (Timber Press), for inspiration anytime. Beautifully produced and luscious to behold, it offers a provocative and refreshing perspective on gardening.

❀ **Admission:** Free.

Garden open: Daily 9:00 A.M. to 7:00 P.M. in spring and summer, 9:00 A.M. to 5:30 P.M. in winter. Call to confirm hours.

Further information: The nursery is wheelchair accessible but not the restroom facilities.

Directions: The nursery is at the corner of West Forty-ninth Avenue and Balaclava Street, 2 blocks below or south of Southwest Marine Drive.

9. Stanley Park

Entrance at north end of Georgia Street, **Vancouver,** BC V6B 4B2; (604) 257–8400; www.parks.vancouver.bc.ca

*I*F YOU come to Vancouver, you must visit the city's vibrant Stanley Park. Named for a former governor-general of Canada, the vast parkland was established in 1886 and opened to the public in 1888.

Worldwide there are few park settings to rival this beautiful urban oasis. Occupying 1,000 acres on a spectacular peninsula setting, Stanley Park offers a wealth of recreational activities as well as a treasure trove for the garden traveler. For a colorful respite during your tour of the park, observe the Ted and Mary Greig Rhododendron Garden's bounteous spring display (near the pitch and putt golf course). Late spring also heralds stunning displays of azaleas, together with flowering cherry and plum trees.

Children take delight in riding the miniature railway, a stunning replica of an early locomotive engine that transports young and old visitors alike on a course through majestic trees. The Children's Farmyard adjacent to the railway is equally appealing.

If your visit happens to fall between April and September, be certain to take in the formal Rose Garden and lavish perennial beds, situated near the Georgia Street entrance to the park. The summertime exhibition encompasses brilliant combinations of annuals grown by the Park Board.

Particularly interesting, Stanley Park's overall habitat exemplifies native West Coast rain-forest vegetation. Composed mainly of second-growth Douglas fir, western hemlock and red cedar, the park's coniferous environment includes fragments of primeval old-growth forest—trees that can exceed 250 feet in height. In contrast to the type of planned and installed landscaping you can expect to encounter in most urban parkland, Stanley Park offers a pristine parcel of the natural world within the city's own boundaries. The park's immense area has regenerated naturally after having been logged in the late nineteenth century.

One of Stanley Park's many compelling pleasures is its Seawall Promenade. Affording unparalleled views, the Seawall path wraps around the park's perimeter for 5 ½ miles, providing lanes for walking, cycling, and in-line skating. Any segment of the Seawall path around the peninsula is a rare treat not to be missed.

On the south side of the park, you'll find the Lost Lagoon and Nature House, where many different bird species consort among the rushes and around the watery preserve. The Nature House's seasonal walking tours should prove informative for anyone with an interest in the natural world.

Ferguson Point is located to the north and west of the lagoon, overlooking English Bay. Here you can enjoy fine dining at the Sequoia Grill, which offers seating in the building's lovely conservatory. At the park's north end, Prospect Point offers fine views of the North Shore mountains and the Lions Gate Bridge.

❀ **Admission:** Free; minimal fee for the children's attractions.

Garden open: Daily dawn to dusk.

Further information: To learn the operating times and route for a free shuttle bus that stops at fourteen of the park's popular attractions, visit the Vancouver Parks' Web site, click on Stanley Park, then click on Shuttle Bus. Note: Vehicular traffic proceeds one-way counterclockwise in the park. Call (604) 257–8531 for the hours of the children's attractions. You can download a map of the park from the Stanley Park Web site link. To enjoy guided walks at the Nature House, managed by the Stanley Park Ecology Society, phone (604) 257–8544 or visit www.stanleyparkecology.ca. You'll find a wide array of choices for meals and snacks, including the Sequoia Grill (formerly known as the Tea House in Stanley Park) on Ferguson Point; phone (800) 280–9893 for reservations. Some trails in this enormous parkland are not wheelchair accessible, but the popular Seawall Promenade is accessible, along with other parts of the park and all its facilities.

Directions: Georgia Street is a major downtown thoroughfare. Entry to the park is at the northern end of Georgia, to the west of the Coal Harbour waterfront and running between the Lost Lagoon and Coal Harbour.

10. University of British Columbia Botanical Garden

6804 Southwest Marine Drive, **Vancouver,** BC V6T 1Z4;
(604) 822–4208, (604) 822–9666 (information line);
www.ubcbotanicalgarden.org

*T*HE UNIVERSITY of British Columbia's seventy-acre botanical garden is a horticultural preserve that has benefited mightily from this Canadian province's climate and coastal conditions. With its fine collections of plants from around the world, the UBC Botanical Garden takes full advantage of a powerful setting overlooking the Strait of Georgia. In an environment where the grandeur of nature largely prevails, captivating plantings pay homage to the beauty of traditional landscaping schemes.

The oldest of Canada's university-affiliated botanical gardens, the University of British Columbia's garden features more than 400 species of rhododendron in one segment of many lovely established garden sections. Blue rhododendrons (*Rhododendron augustinii*) are a particularly outstanding feature of the David C. Lam Asian Garden. Here impressive conifers lend a hushed majesty to the garden's expansive thirty-five acres.

Focusing on species and varieties of Asian origins and highlighting woody plants specifically, the Lam Garden contains disparate flora such as vines and shrubs sheltered by ancient native trees. Grand fir, Douglas fir, western red cedar, and western hemlock all grow in the natural habitat of a second-growth coastal forest. Keep an eye out for bald eagles. They are known to rest atop the botanical garden's towering canopy, so there's a good chance you'll spot one!

Shift your focus back to the level of terra firma, and you will enjoy the Lam Garden's diverse understory of plants. Among the graceful maples, fragrant viburnums, and floriferous clematis, you will find specimens of the rare and hauntingly lovely Snake-bark maples. Three distinct species exhibit green-and-white-striped bark. A host of shade-loving perennials and bulbs, such as the giant lilies (*Cardiocrinum giganteum*), brightens the warmly colored bark mulch pathways.

Resulting in part from heavy rainfall, specimens are endowed with a verdant beauty. Search out the yellow waxbell (*Kirengeshoma koreana*), a member of the Hydrangeaceae plant family, with leaves resembling maples and sensational yellow bell-like flowers possessing a rather plush texture. Less statuesque, the Japanese species *K. palmata* grows here, too, bearing similar blooms. Himalayan blue and Nepal poppies, the distinctive Chinese evergreen oak (*Quercus myrsinifolia*), and countless magnolia species stand out among other rarities. In the garden's beneficial microclimate, you'll witness Himalayan magnolias blooming as early as February.

From the Asian Garden, pass through the striking Moongate and Tunnel to the Food Garden. A pivotal design element is created by espaliered apple trees. They are complemented by a fine collection of fruits, nuts, and vegetables known to grow vigorously in the Vancouver region. Continue on through the handsome arbor. This sizable rustic form provides support for a variety of climbers: wisteria, akebia, American bittersweet (*Celastrus scandens*), and silver lace vine (*Polygonum aubertii*) among them.

The Physick Garden, one of the most distinctive gardens here was inspired by a sixteenth-century Dutch print. Encircling a bronze sundial mounted on a sturdy pedestal, the garden features twelve differentiated shapes devoted to all sorts of fascinating perennial plants selected for their historical associations and medicinal properties. Signs explain ancient usages of these plants. At present the university remains committed to researching the curative powers of certain indigenous plants.

Stroll the expansive E. H. Lohbrunner Alpine Garden, where plants grouped according to continent are agreeably sited on a west-facing incline to partake of the sun's beneficial warmth. A variety of soil conditions are reproduced here to sustain the garden's myriad array of plants, which put forth their most extravagant displays in summertime. Distinguishing the overall design are enchanting floral interplays of delicately colored, diminutive blooms and exhibitions of bulbs. This includes summery show-offs such as red-hot pokers, arising in the African section.

Dramatic foliage contrasts appear to punctuate the garden's rocky paths and outcroppings. The sharply defined shapes of dwarf conifers play off such brilliantly colored specimens as shrubby *Genista pilosa* 'Vancouver Gold'. A popular University of British Columbia Botanical Garden introduction, the cultivated variety of silkyleaf woadwaxen boasts golden leaves and bright yellow flowers.

Yet another revealing garden area gives native plants of British Columbia center stage. Here, and everywhere at the University of British Columbia Botanical Garden, you can admire unparalleled beauty during every season of the year. Of course, while touring the garden, plan also to enjoy a visit to Nitobe Memorial Garden, located just three kilometers (nearly 2 miles) north of the botanical garden.

❀ **Admission:** Fee.

Garden open: Daily 10:00 A.M. to 6:00 P.M. in the summer; call ahead for dates and hours for other seasons. The Shop in the Garden is open during regular hours.

Further information: As a convenience, you can purchase a double-entry ticket to Nitobe Memorial Garden and the UBC Botanical Garden. Visit the Web site to learn about events and attractions at UBC and for details on public transportation, ferries, or parking. You'll find vending machines at the garden, but no food facilities are available. Unusual plants and an array of books and gifts are sold at the Shop in the Garden, situated at the garden's entrance. Phone the shop at

(604) 822-4529. Guided tours are offered to ten people or more; to book, call (604) 822-9666 and leave a message. Parts of the botanical garden are accessible to wheelchairs.

Directions: The botanical garden is on Southwest Marine Drive on the campus of the University of British Columbia in the Point Grey section of Vancouver, which is southwest of downtown. A campus map can be downloaded from the Web site.

11. VanDusen Botanical Garden

5251 Oak Street at Thirty-seventh Avenue, **Vancouver,** BC
V6M 4H1; (604) 878-9274; www.vandusengarden.org

*E*STABLISHED in 1975, VanDusen Botanical Garden features plant collections representing six continents. Located on a southwest Vancouver site, the garden's luxuriant landscape supports an ensemble of forty-six display areas.

Plantings at VanDusen are arranged according to geographical origins as well as botanical associations. Plant lovers will appreciate fascinating displays revealing a kingdom of flora defined by intriguing relationships. To learn more about the garden's myriad plant communities while touring the various sections, visitors can call upon descriptive signs, a Visitor Guide pamphlet, and the *VanDusen Botanical Garden Guidebook.*

Perhaps not obvious to the average garden traveler, VanDusen's lovely lakes, ponds, and streams were originally conceived by garden designers and planners. These attractive water characteristics enhance the landscape. Furthermore, they provide significant habitats for flora and positively impact the ecology of the area by attracting a wealth of fauna to the botanical garden grounds.

Situated just beyond the garden entrance, the Children's Garden aims to entertain with wonderfully contorted woody specimens, topiary beasts, and a bronze replica of Verrochio's *Boy with a Dolphin* found in Florence. If you walk north, the formal Rose Garden (especially outstanding during June and July) and a display of ground covers materialize before you arrive at the garden's acclaimed Laburnum Walk. During May the walk's shrouded arbor is arguably as captivating a sight as you might hope to see on your gardenwalks, for the golden chain trees produce pendulous, opulent golden clusters that create a sensational exhibition.

After you've passed through the Laburnum Walk, the Perennial Garden appears with its enveloping Irish yew hedge and sandstone wall. Enjoyable in June and July when the hostas and hardy geraniums are in bloom, this lovely garden of grasses and flowers perhaps shines brightest in August, when the small space is ornamented by a colorful procession of asters, chrysanthemums, and sedums.

For panoramic views of the city, Coast Range Mountains, and the sea, you must explore the Sino-Himalayan Garden, where the nearly 500-foot summit grants all who pause here an overlook of incredible beauty. Predominately naturalistic in style and shielded by woodland on three sides, the garden is distinguished by rock work and a waterfall. Providing a haven for various rhododendron species that bloom over a period of several months, the Sino-Himalayan Garden presents a gorgeous springtime spectacle of flamboyant flowering magnolias, the fragrant empress tree (*Paulownia tomentosa*), and flashing white bracts of the dove tree (*Davidia involucrata*), looming like fluttery handkerchiefs suspended from innumerable branches. In general, February through early March is a period of bright bloom in this garden and the Rock Garden.

Other VanDusen highlights include sterling collections of hydrangeas and camellias, the largest collection of hollies in Canada, radiant tree peonies, ferns, and heathers. Peaceful copses create additional focal points for species and varieties of oaks, beeches, ashes, maples, true cedars, giant redwoods, and conifers such as yews.

A number of commanding visual markers embellish VanDusen Botanical Garden's admirable botanical assemblage. Here are such unique structural elements as the handsome hexagonal Korean Pavilion; the emerald green Elizabethan Maze, a living foliage design fashioned from 1,000 pyramid cedars (*Thuja occidentalis*); and distinctive stone sculptures placed throughout the gardens. The strong silhouettes of these three-dimensional forms represent yet another exciting aspect of garden.

✤ **Admission:** Fee. Rates vary with the season; call in advance or check the Web site for details.

Garden open: Daily at 10:00 A.M..; closing times vary from month to month. Call or check the Web site for hours of operation. Closed Christmas Day. The Garden Shop is open daily at 10:00 A.M. Shaughnessy Restaurant opens at 11:30 A.M. (see below).

Further information: Call to confirm times for guided walking tours, taking place daily at 2:00 P.M.; free with admission. You'll find special events listed on the Web site should you wish to attend a lecture or plant sale. If you plan to visit in June, be sure to check the Web site well in advance for details on the VanDusen Garden Show, which covers fifteen acres in the Great Lawn area. Tickets for this delightful event can be purchased online. Look for gift items with a horticultural theme, from books and tools to clothing and footwear, in the garden shop, located in the Entrance Pavilion. Call (604) 257–8665 for information. Call the Shaughnessy Restaurant at (604) 261–0011 for reservations. Lunch, afternoon tea, and dinner are served. For wheelchair-accessible routes that take in the high points of the Garden, ask for a wheeled route map from the cashier.

Directions: VanDusen Botanical Garden is located in the heart of the city, at the corner of Thirty-seventh Avenue, between Oak and Granville Streets; about ten minutes by car from the downtown area.

Vancouver Island Gardenwalks

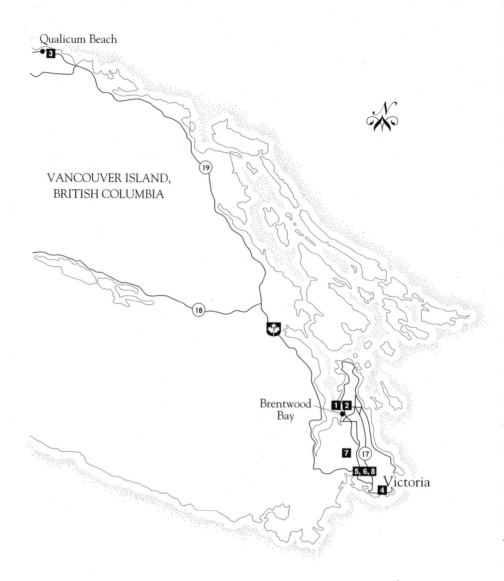

Qualicum Beach

VANCOUVER ISLAND,
BRITISH COLUMBIA

N

Brentwood
Bay

Victoria

1. The Butchart Gardens

800 Benvenuto Avenue, **Brentwood Bay,** BC
(mailing address: Box 4010, Victoria, BC V8X 3X4);
(866) 652–4422, (250) 652–5256 (recorded message),
(250) 652–4422 (business office); www.butchartgardens.com

*W*HEN Robert Pim Butchart and his imaginative wife, Jennie,
set about transforming the Butchart portland cement quarry
into the remarkable sunken garden that captivates today's visitors,
it was a stupendous undertaking! If it's color you crave—of nearly
unimaginable magnitude—visit Vancouver Island's enchanting city
of Victoria to tour the Butchart Gardens.

These impressive gardens stand as a wonderful commemora-
tion of the couple's generous spirit and pay tribute to their enduring
marriage. In this glorious setting, you can feel Jennie Butchart's
boundless energy and Robert Butchart's enterprising spirit. His grand-
son, R. Ian Ross, remained active as chief steward until his death in
1997. The Butchart Gardens are currently owned by members of the
Ross/Butchart family.

Begun in the early days of the twentieth century, the Butchart
Gardens encompass fifty-five lush acres open to the public (part of
a 130-acre estate), overflowing with blooms both delightfully com-
monplace and intriguingly rare. A visit here affords glimpses of such
treasures as the coveted Tibetan blue poppy (*Meconopsis betonici-
folia baileyii*) that has graced these gardens since the 1920s. At the
same time you'll behold exaggerated vistas, where fastidious lawns
surround seemingly endless drifts of familiar summer annuals, put
together in rousing rainbows of multicolored zinnias, startling red
salvias, and tuberous begonias of all shades and hues. Gaillardias,

godetias, and of course marigolds grow unrestrained within asymmetrically shaped beds and sweeping borders.

A tremendous source of pleasure for countless visitors from decades past, the gardens attract more than one million visitors yearly, and they continue to draw present-day garden travelers to this lovely region of the Pacific Northwest. As seasons change, the Butchart Gardens reveal a shifting garden spectacle. The beauty of a rare snowfall accents the subtle fanfare of witch hazels and hollies, heathers and hellebores. The winter appeal of such plants ranges from the refined flowers to the interesting foliage textures and branching forms. Each year more than 250,000 new bulbs are imported from Holland to light up the gardens in spring, when blankets of snowdrops are followed by unparalleled exhibitions of scillas, showy daffodils, and grand expanses of tulips from February through April. With the arrival of May, heaps of anemone and ranunculus emerge. Various rhododendrons bloom from March through June, turning pristine walkways into veritable wonderlands of radiant color!

A summer promenade at the Butchart Gardens should take you past the handsome Rose Garden, with bush roses, standards, and vigorous climbers drenched in blooms. Roses start blooming around the beginning of June and flower through September. Arresting stands of delphiniums highlight the flowing circular design. Continue exploring and enjoy the gardens' fountains and ponds for a refreshing contrast. A lovely pool anchors the Italian Garden's formal symmetry while, nearby, the Japanese Garden provides a more rarefied setting. Pause here to admire the fine ornamentation and striking bridges combined with elegant trees, shrubs, and lovely associations of foliage.

The fragile yet graceful American trout lily, towering stalks of joe-pye weed (*Eupatorium*), and lovely queen of the prairie (*Filipendula*) are examples of the stunning perennial plantings at the Butchart Gardens. For lovers of the dramatic, nighttime illumination ignites the gardens' great masses of annuals as well as such strong vertical elements like tall conifers and the feathery forms of deciduous trees. During the months of July and August, the gardens are aglow with the additional excitement of music and entertainment.

All who favor autumn above other seasons should come in October and admire the dazzling fall colors of Japanese maples and liquidambar trees, Boston ivy, purple beech, and golden locust. During the holidays there is special entertainment at Christmastime, and buildings and grounds are lavishly decorated and lit in festive style for a visually stimulating experience.

❁ **Admission:** Fee.

Garden open: Daily 9:00 A.M.; closing times vary seasonally. Gates open at 1:00 P.M. on Christmas Day. Phone in advance or check the Web site for closing times. The Giftstore and Information Centre remain open one hour after the gate closing.

Further information: Special entertainment and seasonal attractions are listed on the Web site, along with garden news and the best visiting times. Tickets can be purchased online. Families can enjoy casual meals at the Blue Poppy Restaurant, which serves meals cafeteria-style. The Coffee Shop offers boxed lunches and lighter fare; you'll find cappuccino, pastries, and ice cream at the Soda Fountain. Phone (250) 652–8222 for fine-dining reservations at the Dining Room Restaurant. Buildings and gardens are wheelchair accessible; however, paths are less crowded early in the morning or after 3:00 P.M. Stairs can be avoided by following specific paths indicated on the map given out upon admission. Some pathways can be steep, such as in the Japanese Garden.

Directions: The Butchart Gardens are 22 kilometers (14 miles) north of Victoria and 20 kilometers (12½ miles) south of the Vancouver–

Victoria Ferry terminal at Swartz Bay. See the Web site for detailed transportation information, maps, and direct driving routes.

Traveling along the British Columbia Coast

British Columbia Ferry Services Inc.—known as BC Ferries—provides service to nearly fifty ports of call along the coast of British Columbia. When planning a trip, you may find it helpful to refer to maps of ferry routes or schedules found at www.bcferries .com. You can also make reservations online.

To discover what's happening in Vancouver or on Vancouver Island, look over the events calendar on BC Ferries' Web site. You'll find an informative overview of ongoing exhibits, upcoming tourism highlights, and seasonal celebrations. Suggested destinations in the fall, for example, include a visit to Victoria's Goldstream Provincial Park, where you can see the salmon spawning and take in the setting's ancient firs, red cedars and yews. Another possibility is a sojourn to the annual Christmas festivities at the Butchart Gardens.

The Web site also offers driving directions to the various ferry terminals, fares, and current conditions for the ferries; detailed information on regional bus service connecting Vancouver and Vancouver Island; travel planning; and assistance with hotels and car rentals.

You don't need online access to contact BC Ferries. Write to them at 1112 Fort Street, Victoria, BC V8V 4V2. To make a ferry reservation from outside British Columbia, call (250) 286-3431 any day of the year from 7:00 A.M. to 10:00 P.M. Pacific time. Call toll-free from anywhere in British Columbia by dialing (888) 223-3779.

2. Victoria Butterfly Gardens

1461 Benvenuto Avenue, **Brentwood Bay,** BC V8M 1R3;
(877) 722–0272; www.butterflygardens.com

$\mathcal{J}$F YOU ENJOY taking photos, have your camera ready and plenty of film on hand. A visit to the Victoria Butterfly Gardens may be what you're looking for, with its exotic birds, waterfalls, and the magic of fluttering butterflies animating a 12,000-square-foot rain-forest environment and wonderland of tropical plants.

Spectacular angel's trumpets (*Brugmansia*) are among the showy ornamentals displayed here, but you'll also see specific host plants like Dutchman's-pipe, where the butterflies lay their eggs, and nectar plants that supply a food source necessary for the butterflies to reproduce.

An 80-foot wall covered in passion vines is a sight. In addition to the blue crown passionflower (*Passiflora caerulea*) and *P. biflora*, look for the vermilion flowers of *P. vitifolia*. A woody vine native to Central and South America, *Allamanda* is a vigorous beauty cloaked in evergreen leaves and accented by golden trumpet-shaped blooms.

Seek out the epiphyte section, with its bevy of orchid blooms peaking from July into October. A carnivorous bog is mysterious and intriguing.

❀ **Admission:** Fee.

Garden open: Daily from March to October. Opening and closing times vary; phone for dates and times.

Further information: Visit the Web site to enjoy virtual tours of the gardens and gift shop. A restaurant and deli are in the same building; menus can be found on the Web site. The gardens are wheelchair accessible.

Directions: The gardens are about twenty minutes north of Victoria on the corner of West Saanich and Keating X Road, less than five minutes from the Butchart Gardens.

3. Milner Gardens and Woodland

2179 West Island Highway, **Qualicum Beach,** BC V9K 1G1;
(250) 752–6153 (reservations and information),
(250) 752–8573 (administration); www.milnergardens.org

*I*N A DRAMATIC coastal setting graced with a noble sixty-acre forest, Milner Gardens and Woodland include a ten-acre heritage garden and a beguiling, wisteria-draped house.

Given to Malaspina University-College in 1996, the gardens were initially developed by philanthropist Ray Milner and his first wife, Rina, who passed away in 1952. Mr. Milner married Veronica Fitzgerald in 1954, a formidable woman with a talent for oil painting and an impressive knowledge of horticulture.

Over a span of more than forty years, Veronica applied her artistic vision to the selection of the gardens' exceptional collection of woody plants, creating a landscape in harmony with its surroundings. On a personal note, her aristocratic family ties extended to Prime Minister Winston Churchill and to Princess Diana, one of the estate's many illustrious guests.

The present-day existence of Milner Gardens is of great significance, as the property and adjacent parcels constitute a rare example of an old-growth forest made up of Douglas and grand firs and western red cedars.

Designed by A. N. Fraser and constructed between 1929 and 1931, the Milner house exhibits a delightful profile inspired by the concept of a Ceylonese tea plantation house. Elements such as handsome gables defined by painted trim and screened doors showing the way into the garden distinguish the design.

Renovations and changes to the house in later years resulted in the gracious building that awaits today's visitors. In addition to housing offices, a library, and display cases containing historical photographs and documents, the Milner house offers rooms the public can enjoy, including the dining room, drawing room, and other parts of the lovely interior. Refreshments served in the Camellia Tea Room are accompanied by views of the garden, ocean, and mountains.

The Milner Gardens take advantage of the sheltered, temperate conditions on the east coast of Vancouver Island, situated in the rain shadow of the island's mountain range.

From the Welcome Center an interpretive trail leads through the forest. Entering the gardens to begin your tour, a native pond and large open meadow lend character to the scenery as you veer left, going toward the Pool House (this is the drop-off point for the shuttle cart).

If you proceed directly ahead toward the Milner house, your approach reveals a rhododendron glade on the left, before you reach the Gardener's Cottage. In springtime you'll find the garden atmosphere punctuated by brilliant displays of rhododendrons: An impressive 400 varieties grow here.

Continuing on to the house, an array of viburnums appears alongside the pathway.

Outside the Tea Room, adorning the house, you'll discover a fine alliance of camellias, with their glossy leaves and lush flowers. Look for the rose garden to emerge nearby.

Deciduous azaleas put on a show across the lawn, while a bit farther along, you'll find eye-catching compositions in a lovely display of perennials.

As the seasons unfold, the scent of honeysuckle drifts on the air, and elegant lace-cap hydrangeas bolster the surroundings.

Visit in fall and you'll be swept away by autumnal hues that drench the garden in a sea of tantalizing gold, orange, coral, and burnished red set off by the emerald tones of evergreens. This artful palette of foliage takes in a handsome array of trees: maples and beeches as well as *Davidia*, stewartia, and katsura specimens.

The gardens' captivating site features a spectacular bluff descending to the beach below, together with stunning vistas across the Strait of Georgia to the Coast Range Mountains of British Columbia in the distance. Wildlife, too, animates the scenery, from bald eagles and herons to tiny wrens and colorful finches.

✿ **Admission:** Fee.

Garden open: From Mother's Day to Labor Day: daily 10:00 A.M. to 5:00 P.M. April 1 to May 1 and September 8 to October 10: Thursday through Sunday and holiday Mondays 10:00 A.M. to 5:00 P.M. Call to confirm hours. The Pool House Gift Shop is open during regular garden hours. The Tea Room is open 1:00 to 4:00 P.M.

Further information: Look for the Monthly Flower Report, found on the Web site along with a listing of special programs and events. The Tea Room seats forty people and serves on a first-come, first-serve basis. Light refreshments are also served at the gift shop, where you can relax on the patio or next to the pool. The gardens are mostly wheelchair accessible, but not the nature trail, where taking the road down is an option. A golf cart driven by volunteers can transport anyone with mobility challenges in and out of the garden.

Directions: Milner Gardens are approximately two and a half hours north of Victoria; forty minutes north of Nanaimo. Take Highway 19 north to the Qualicum Beach exit. Go straight on Memorial Avenue to the water; turn right onto West Island Highway (Highway 19A). Proceed about 2 kilometers (1 1/4 miles) to Milner Gardens.

4. Abkhazi Garden

1964 Fairfield Road, **Victoria,** BC V8S 1H4;
(250) 598–8096; www.conservancy.bc.ca

$\mathcal{I}$N A SECTION of the city not far removed from lovely downtown Victoria, the Abkhazi Garden takes in approximately
one acre, yet its beauty resonates with the impact of a garden on a
grander scale.

The history of the garden encompasses aspects of tragedy, drama,
and romance. Its creators, Marjorie Pemberton-Carter and Georgian

The Land Conservancy

The Land Conservancy (TLC) is a nonprofit organization
inspired by Great Britain's National Trust. Throughout British
Columbia, TLC works to preserve plant habitats and safeguard
scenic sites. In protecting the natural and cultural heritage of the
entire province, TLC cares for noteworthy buildings and archaeological sites as well as grasslands and riparian environments.

Abkhazi Garden in Victoria is one of the exceptional
properties under the auspices of TLC. To learn about other
noteworthy conservation projects, visit the Web site www
.conservancy.bc.ca and click on Properties and Projects. From
there you can search the "Find a Property" feature and view gardens, nature sanctuaries, and other landscapes with unique ecological characteristics. Peruse the individual listings to determine
what workshops, guided walks, and other activities might be
scheduled during your journey to the area, or look on the home
page for a listing of current and upcoming events. At Abkhazi
Garden, for instance, a flower-arranging demonstration or a series
of artists' lectures may be scheduled.

TLC's head office is at 2709 Shoreline Drive, Victoria, BC
V9B 1M5; (250) 479–8053. Other regional offices are listed on
the Web site.

Prince Nicholas Abkhazi, met in Paris in the 1920s. Each suffered personal losses early in life. And each came to be interned in prison camps during the Second World War: Peggy in China and Nicholas in Germany. Reunited in 1946, they married and went on to develop their exceptional Vancouver Island garden over four decades.

On a tour of the garden, you will encounter a rocky site presided over by native Garry oaks. Its current transformation is distinguished by characteristic divisions.

A woodland garden celebrates rhododendrons, both species and hybrid varieties, with many venerable specimens having developed into magnificent trees. You can expect to find plants in bloom here as early as January, and late bloomers carry on into June. A host of delicate companion plantings thread through, introducing a realm of magical blooms: fawn lily, trillium, and jack-in-the-pulpit (*Arisaema*) among them. The imposing Himalayan lily (*Cardiocrinum*) is outstanding in summer, together with hostas, primroses, and uncommon ferns.

Bathed in sun, the South Lawn's layout currently boasts a soothing naturalism, from beds filled with flowering shrubs to a path pointing the way to craggy rock formations that function as part of the house's unyielding foundation. Look for an exuberant border filled with summer performers with interesting architecture. An original hornbeam hedge serves to set off plants with silvery leaves, an effective homage to a superb rock situated nearby.

Continuing along, gaze at the stirring view, looking beyond the rocks to the landscape's uppermost boundary, where another garden room awaits.

The restored summerhouse is yet another highlight within the richly textured terrain. A charming structure, it emerges as a beacon, exemplifying its artful designation as a focal point.

Expect to be surprised and delighted by many additional features when you tour the lyrical setting of the Abkhazi Garden. It exists today for all to enjoy, thanks to the efforts of the Land Conservancy of British Columbia, which stepped in and rescued the property in 2000 when it was slated to be sold for development.

❀ **Admission:** Fee.

Garden open: From March through September 30. Wednesday through Sunday and holidays 1:00 to 5:00 P.M.

Further information: The Land Conservancy Web site provides additional background on the Abkhazi Garden, along with detailed directions to the garden via car or public transportation. The garden also can be visited in conjunction with the Garden Conservancy's Open Days Program; see the listing in the resources chapter. Wheelchair access is limited.

Directions: Abkhazi Garden is in the Fairfield neighborhood of Victoria. Travel south on Blanshard Street, turning left onto Fairfield Road. Continue past Foul Bay Road; the garden is directly to the east.

5. Beacon Hill Park

Dallas Road, between Cook and Douglas Streets, **Victoria**, BC; (250) 361–0600; www.city.victoria.bc.ca

WIDELY KNOWN as the City of Gardens, Victoria is endowed with an urban space that is truly its crowning glory: Beacon Hill Park.

Burial grounds discovered in the park have indicated the significance of this wondrous landscape to Native peoples, including

Herons Online

Beacon Hill Park in Victoria is a birder's paradise. It provides a rare domicile for great blue herons. Look for these elegant birds when you visit the park. Or log on to www.heroncam.com to get glimpses of these remarkable birds.

the Songhees Indians. The history of Beacon Hill Park traces its European heritage to 1850, while the 178-acre setting of today captivates nature lovers and garden travelers alike.

Here you will find something to appreciate year-round, from a native Garry oak ecosystem where swaths of wildflowers bloom in spring to charming diversions such as a genteel nineteenth-century garden of ornamentals.

Enjoy strolling to the high point of Beacon Hill, meandering across the sloping meadowland to majestic cliffs overlooking the beaches along Dallas Road.

Or walk along the Dallas Road Waterfront, where the waterfront walk spans Holland Point to Clover Point. Here you'll encounter a perimeter of parkland fronting Dallas Road; across from the park is Finlayson Point. You'll discover there is nothing to impede the breathtaking views of the Juan de Fuca Strait and magnificent Olympic Mountains.

On Camas Day, taking place in April, heaps of the beautiful blue flowers burst forth, luring visitors to the park. Areas blanketed with naturalized daffodils are another delightful sight.

The alluring character of the park's refined inner area is a joy to behold at any time. A Victorian garden scene, it boasts lovely lawns, picturesque bridges reaching across idyllic streams and man-made lakes, and richly textured plant combinations.

Throughout the summer freshly planted specimens vivify flower beds: salvias and lobelias, marigolds and begonias. A wealth of handsome trees adds to the inviting atmosphere, and musical performances in the Cameron Bandshell are further inducements to drop by on a summer's evening.

In the autumn, summer plants are replaced with hardy plants and those that will bloom the following spring, such as primroses and wallflowers. And woody shrubs, including rhododendrons, offer an effective flush of blooms whatever the season.

Look for the Mile 0 marker: It observes the westernmost point of the Trans-Canada Highway. Doubtless you'll find other garden travelers documenting the spot with a photograph.

✿ **Admission:** Free.

Garden open: Daily, around-the-clock. The parking lot at the top of Beacon Hill is open dawn to dusk.

Further information: The Friends of Beacon Hill Park have put together an informative Web site that you will want to visit: www .friendsofbeaconhillpark.ca. Wheelchair accessibility varies within this large park.

Directions: Beacon Hill Park is on Dallas Road between Cook and Douglas Streets, directly south and within walking distance of downtown Victoria. Follow Douglas Street as it runs south along the park's western periphery.

6. Government House Gardens

1401 Rockland Avenue, **Victoria,** BC V8S 1V9;
www.ltgov.bc.ca

*I*N THIS heritage residential area you'll find "the ceremonial home of all British Columbians," Government House, with its lovely granite facade in shades of gray, blue, and pink. And its terraces and balconies are set off by black slate paving as further embellishment.

The thirty-five-acre property encompasses some fourteen acres of exemplary formal gardens. You'll delight in exploring the English Country Garden situated inside the Main Gate. Flowering displays of perennials, bulbs, and traditional cottage garden plants are a highlight.

A Sunken Rose Garden appears near the Herb Garden, on the western side of the property. Expect to be swept away by fragrant specimens of David Austin English roses. A perfect complement to the roses, the Herb Garden shows off the soft blues and grays of medicinal and culinary varieties. Medlar and quince trees accent the plantings.

Between the Fountain Pond and the Central Gate, look for a vibrant mixed border known as Rockland Border 1, running parallel to Rockland Avenue. The textural melding of grasses and bulbs creates an alluring composition. Another border, extending to the Trades Gate, demonstrates beautiful plant combinations for a shady setting. Uncommon hostas and hydrangeas come together here as exceptional allies.

Be sure to allot enough time for your visit, because there is much to discover. A gazebo and pergola adorn an admirable layout in the Victorian Rose Garden. The Bruce Pavilion is enhanced by fine ironwork. The gardens seem to go on and on, with displays of rhododendrons and irises, a Rock and Alpine Garden, a Heather Garden, and more.

❀ **Admission:** Free.

Garden open: Daily sunrise to sunset.

Further information: Visit the Web site to read a detailed history of the building and the earlier residences that once stood in its place. The Friends of Government House Gardens Society provides a brochure of tour information that can be downloaded off the Web site, or phone (250) 356–5139 for further information on garden tours. Garden areas are wheelchair accessible.

Directions: Stroll east from downtown Victoria and the Inner Harbour, and you'll reach the gardens in about twenty-five minutes. Look on the Web site for a detailed map and public transit information.

7. The Horticulture Centre

505 Quayle Road, **Victoria**, BC V9E 2J7; (250) 479–6162; www.hcp.bc.ca

*I*DLE AWAY a day at the Horticulture Centre and you're certain to come away refreshed. Established in 1979 as a not-for-profit society by a group of Victoria-area residents, the center stands out as a noteworthy resource for gardeners of the Pacific Northwest as well as a horticultural attraction for garden travelers. Situated in a lovely rural Vancouver Island locale outside the city of Victoria, the Horticulture Centre has more than one hundred acres of unspoiled natural areas and cultivated demonstration gardens.

Approximately five acres are devoted to a variety of specialty gardens, including a substantial trial garden for dahlias, the Doris Page Winter Garden displaying hundreds of plants that thrive in USDA Zone 8, and the Takata Japanese Garden. The center's principal gardens are found in front of the entrance area, where the landscape and plantings extend invitingly in the direction of a lake. An exuberant collection of shrubs, trees, and borders bursting with perennials and annuals indicates choice selections for Victoria-area gardens. Hardy fuchsias, heathers, and Michaelmas daisies are highlights.

The Horticulture Centre remains committed to preserving a large segment of primarily undeveloped land. Sheltered within the ninety-acre parcel of this untouched landscape is an area of wetlands and a section where native plants such as Garry oak flourish. A carefully designed trail system allows visitors to observe but not disturb the fragile Garry oak and wetland habitat. This conservation park is currently being rehabilitated as a functioning Douglas-fir ecosystem. Dozens of varieties of birds take refuge here as well.

The center engages in and promotes research and sponsors educational activities such as talks and classes on various garden topics. It also supports a trade school specializing in the training of maintenance gardeners.

Whenever you happen to be touring the area, you can count on memorable gardenwalks and relaxing vistas at the Horticulture Centre. There are always new and expanding gardens thanks to the participation and nurture of 1,300 local members from surrounding communities. One of the best times to visit is during the bleak days of winter, as the winter garden blooms from December to March. A lovely spring show follows in the rhododendron garden.

❀ **Admission:** Fee; free for children under 16.
    Garden open: Daily 8:00 A.M. to 8:00 P.M. in summer, 9:00 A.M. to 4:00 P.M. in winter. Phone to confirm hours.
    Further information: You can enjoy a self-guided tour during open hours. Guided tours are by appointment only for groups of ten or more and must be booked in advance. A fee is charged for each tour group of ten to fifteen visitors. You'll find a calendar of special events on the Web site. Wheelchair access is limited, and some pathways are steep.
    Directions: The center is off West Saanich Road, 12 kilometers (7½ miles) north of downtown Victoria. Contact the center for detailed directions.

8. Victoria's Hanging Baskets

Located throughout the Inner Harbour and downtown Victoria; (250) 361–0600; www.city.victoria.bc.ca

For more than sixty years, the city of Victoria has maintained a tradition of lavishly planted hanging baskets that appear on lampposts downtown in early June each year to celebrate summer's arrival. They remain in place until the end of September.

The first baskets heralded the seventy-fifth anniversary of Victoria's incorporation; the year was 1937.

Plant material for the baskets is grown in the city's own Beacon Hill Nursery. Look at the baskets in sunny areas, and you'll see vibrant plant combinations made up of vigorous varieties such as *Geranium* 'Shirley Claret' and *Petunia* 'Rose Madness' playing off *Lobelia* 'Fountain Blue' and *Lobelia* 'Sapphire'. Plants like lamium provide variegation and texture.

Victoria's Arboreal Display

Victoria offers another citywide visual feast in addition to its famous hanging baskets ornamenting thousands of lampposts. From late February to the end of May, the blooms of distinctive boulevard trees brighten Victoria's streets. Flowering plums and cherries strut their stuff early on, followed by such stunning specimens as magnolias and billowy, double pink Higan cherries. Then the crabapples, dogwoods, horse chestnuts, and later-blooming cherry trees put on a show that merits kudos.

More recently, baskets have featured plantings for shade as well. Impatiens varieties brighten these baskets, along with lovely, trailing Rhodochiton.

More than 1,000 baskets are included in the program, so you can imagine how the city's boulevards and streets are enlivened when these hanging bouquets appear.

Shopkeepers and businesses have followed the city's lead, adding their own ebullient baskets to the display. It's a beautification program known worldwide, and one that rightly draws tourists to Victoria.

❀ **Admission:** Free.

Garden open: Daily from the second week of June through the end of September.

Further information: Walkways in the downtown area are wheelchair accessible.

Directions: Baskets are placed on the city's distinctive lampposts throughout the Inner Harbour Walkway and downtown streets. For more details, contact City of Victoria Parks and Recreation Department, # 1 Centennial Square, Victoria, BC V8W 1P6.

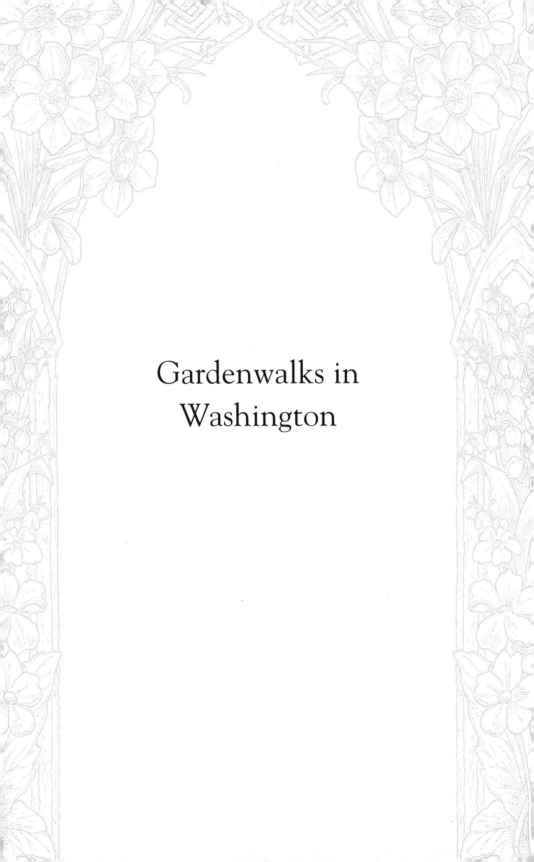

Gardenwalks in Washington

Whatcom County and
Whidbey Island Gardenwalks

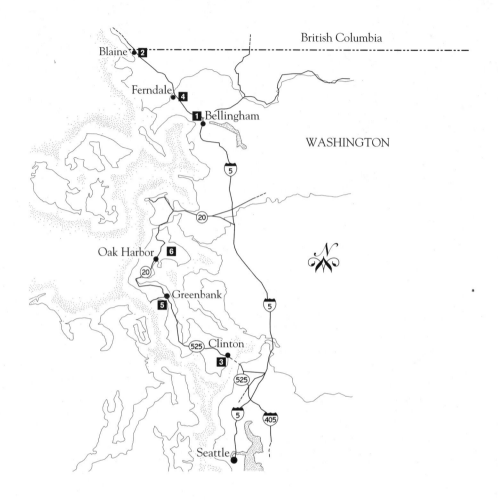

Blaine ●2
British Columbia
Ferndale ●4
1● Bellingham
WASHINGTON
5
20
Oak Harbor ●6
20
5● Greenbank
N
525 Clinton
●3
525
5 405
Seattle ●

1. Bellingham: Sehome Hill
   Arboretum
2. Blaine: Peace Arch State Park
3. Clinton: Cultus Bay Nursery
   & Garden
4. Ferndale: Fragrance
   Garden at Tennant Lake
   Interpretive Center and
   Hovander Homestead Park

5. Greenbank: Meerkerk
   Rhododendron Gardens
6. Oak Harbor: Hummingbird Farm
   Nursery and Gardens

1. Sehome Hill Arboretum

Twenty-fifth Street off Bill McDonald Parkway,
Bellingham, WA 98225; (360) 676–6985;
www.ac.wwu.edu/~sha, www.cob.org/parks

ESTERN Washington University and the City of Bellingham manage this 165-acre preserve, with its refreshing hiking trails for observation of native flora, wildlife, and a thriving bird population.

Conifers dominate the arboretum's forested surroundings; primarily Douglas firs together with lesser numbers of western hemlocks and western red cedars. In open areas that receive more light, you'll come upon big-leaf maples and alders, while the understory shrubbery is dense with Oregon grape, Indian plum, and snowberry.

All the gravel hiking trails lead to an 80-foot observation tower. It stands as a lookout point over the city of Bellingham, the San Juan Islands, Mount Baker, and the surrounding mountain ranges. Vigorous nature lovers who pick a clear day to trek to the top of Sehome Hill will be rewarded with stunning views.

Admission: Free.

Garden open: Daily dawn to dusk.

Further information: Wheelchair accessibility is limited.

Directions: The arboretum is located south of downtown Bellingham in the Sehome Hill neighborhood, above the campus of Western Washington University. Follow Interstate 5 and take the Samish Way exit to the Bill MacDonald Parkway. You'll find parking at the arboretum's south entrance.

2. Peace Arch State Park

Boundary of the United States and Canada at Interstate 5
(mailing address: P.O. Box 87, **Blaine**, WA 98230);
(800) 233–0321; www.parks.wa.gov

CELEBRATING the peaceful relationship between the United States and its neighbor to the north, the Peace Arch State Park Heritage Site focuses attention on a monumental central feature—a 67-foot concrete arch built to reach across the border of the two countries.

With its moorings firmly rooted in American and Canadian soil, the Peace Arch is surrounded by a lovely twenty-acre landscape maintained jointly by Washington State and British Columbia.

The park boasts an interpretive trail where you can enjoy a short hike, picnic tables, good bird-watching, and a children's play area.

Expansive lawns, dignified mature oaks, and summer plantings of showy annuals confirm that horticulture also rates high on a list of the park's attributes. Look for flower gardens interspersed throughout the parkland. Compelling displays in springtime yield the myriad colors of rhododendrons and azaleas set off by textural heathers, while the turning leaves of poplar, birch, maple, and cherry trees contribute to a blaze of color that lights up the grounds in fall.

A stopover at this scenic locale affords wonderful vistas of Semiahmoo Bay and takes in Point Roberts, Vancouver to Vancouver Island, and the San Juans.

Admission: Fee required for a vehicle parking permit.
Garden open: Daily 8:00 A.M. to dusk.
Further information: This is a day-use-only park, with wheelchair access.
Directions: The park is 21 miles north of Bellingham. Interstate 5 bisects the park; take I–5 north to exit 276—the final exit before entering Canada—and follow signs to Peace Arch State Park.

Skagit Valley in Spring

Many garden travelers plan to visit Washington's Skagit Valley in springtime. If you're in the area, drop by Roozengaarde Flowers & Bulbs in Mount Vernon and take in their three-acre Show Garden, abloom during early spring (generally through April) with tulips and daffodils.

Look for the Field Bloom Update on Roozengaarde's Web site at www.tulips.com. You can track bloom status for the affiliated Washington Bulb Company's countless acres of flowering bulbs. You'll find a detailed "bloom map," indicating what's in bloom in the fields during the growing season. A calendar of events lists special happenings throughout the year (in summer you can enjoy a picnic on the grounds), along with month-by-month open hours for the Roozengaarde Gift Shop. Roozengaarde is located approximately one hour north of Seattle, off Interstate Highway 5. Write to them at 15867 Beaver Marsh Road, Mount Vernon, WA 98273; or call (360) 424–8531 or (800) 732–3266.

Springtime also brings the annual Skagit Valley Tulip Festival. For information about the festival, log on www.tulipfestival.org.

3. Cultus Bay Nursery & Garden

7568 Cultus Bay Road, **Clinton,** WA 98236; (360) 579–2329; www.cultusbaynursery.com

*H*OW THANKFUL I was that Dan Hinkley of Heronswood Nursery suggested I visit Mary Fisher's Cultus Bay Nursery on Whidbey Island. A terrific place to explore unusual plant offerings, the Cultus Bay property features exuberant display gardens in the midst of a fine retail nursery. You'll also find Mary's family home—a lovely Victorian-style house surrounded by a luxuriant landscape of charming hedgerows and a profusion of perennials, vines, herbs, and shrubs.

In late August I was captivated by the nursery's densely planted fanfare of blooming herbs, drought-tolerant plantings, and the exceptional exhibition of buddleias and hydrangeas. The thriving gardens were complemented by a selection of unusual, one-of-a-kind garden ornaments.

Always on the lookout for variegated specimens, I was thrilled to find both a stunning porcelainberry vine (*Ampelopsis brevipedunculata* 'Elegans') and the goldnet honeysuckle (*Lonicera japonica* 'Aureoreticulata') for my new California garden.

❀ **Admission:** Free

Garden open: Thursday through Monday 10:00 A.M. to 5:00 P.M. from April through September. Call to confirm hours. Open off-season by appointment only.

Further information: Visit the web site to learn about special events, to view a map, or for detailed directions to the nursery. Paths are not paved, but they are flat and accessible to wheelchairs.

Directions: Cultus Bay Nursery is located on the south end of Whidbey Island, at the intersection of Cultus Bay Road and Bailey Road, just minutes south of Clinton Ferry Dock. From Seattle, drive north on I–5, and take the exit to the Mukilteo–Clinton Ferry. The nursery is about an hour and a half from Seattle. From the Mukilteo–Clinton Ferry, take Highway 525 to the Ken's Korner intersection and turn left onto Cultus Bay Road.

4. Fragrance Garden at Tennant Lake Interpretive Center and Hovander Homestead Park

5236 Nielsen Road, **Ferndale,** WA 98248; (360) 384–3064 (Interpretive Center); (360) 884–3444 (Fragrance Garden and Hovander Homestead Park); www.co.whatcom.wa.us/parks

*T*HE TENNANT LAKE Interpretive Center features Nielsen House, a natural history facility focusing on the Tennant Lake environment. The center offers special hands-on experiences for children, while the Tennant Lake elevated boardwalk provides an excellent chance for everyone to explore a wetland habitat. Designed as a 1-mile loop, the trail facilitates observation points throughout the center's marshlands and features a tower station for optimum viewing. A telescope positioned at ground level within the tower helps to bring the flora and fauna to center stage.

Next to the Interpretive Center, a Fragrance Garden features more than 200 choice flowers and herbs designed especially for the enjoyment of the visually impaired. A visit here is best enjoyed from mid-May to mid-August.

A wheelchair-accessible connector trail links the Tennant Lake Interpretive Center to the adjacent Hovander Homestead Park, another highlight of this Whatcom County recreation complex. The historic park, located at 5299 Nielsen Road, includes acres of farmland amid a lovely riverside setting along the Nooksack River. Flower and vegetable gardens and an orchard surround the turn-of-the-twentieth-century Hovander House. An enormous, iconic red barn with farm animals and antique equipment can be enjoyed here. Plan your visit to include a picnic, and take advantage of one of the sites with superb views of Mount Baker.

❈ **Admission:** Free

Garden open: Daily sunrise to sunset for Hovander Homestead Park and the Fragrance Garden; call for hours for Hovander House. Tennant Lake Interpretive Center is open noon to 4:00 P.M. Thursday through Saturday and on Sunday in summer; call to confirm days and hours before visiting. The boardwalk is closed from mid-September through mid-January.

Further information: Enjoy self-guided tours of these attractions. Contact Whatcom County Parks and Recreation at (360) 733–2900 for more details. Hovander House is not wheelchair accessible. Hovander Homestead Park, the Interpretive Center, and the Fragrance Garden are wheelchair accessible.

Directions: Take the Ferndale turnoff (exit 262) off I–5, go west to the railroad underpass and immediately turn left. Turn right onto Nielsen Road and follow signs to the park. Look on the Web site for a map.

5. Meerkerk Rhododendron Gardens

3531 Meerkerk Lane, **Greenbank**, WA 98253; (360) 678–1912; www.meerkerkgardens.org

*W*HIDBEY ISLAND is a tranquil and beautiful Pacific Northwest locale and a popular destination point. Investigate the horticultural richness of the 48-mile-long island located north of Seattle, and you'll understand why it holds such special appeal for garden lovers.

Situated around the island's geographical midpoint, in Greenbank, you'll find the Meerkerk Rhododendron Gardens. At one time the private gardens of Ann and Max Meerkerk, the gardens are currently operated under the auspices of the Seattle Rhododendron Society and with the help of American Rhododendron Society volunteers, Island County master gardeners, and local garden clubs. Meerkerk Gardens' ten acres of display gardens thrive within the enfolding Meerkerk Woodland Preserve, which stretches over some forty-three acres.

Garden travelers are lured here by the thousands of rhododendrons, flowering trees, bulbs, and newer perennial plantings, which create inspiring displays especially from April to mid-May. By contrast the forested surroundings (incorporating 5 miles of nature trails) evoke a reverent admiration for the pristine scenery. The gardens' peaceful atmosphere is perfect for relaxed walks through fine botanical collections.

The Asian Garden section highlights exotic rhododendron species propagated from seed, including tree-form specimens.

The International Test Garden for hybrid rhododendrons offers a chance to make comparisons between new varieties and the diverse species and cultivars growing throughout the gardens. Look for the lush double flowers, bicolors, and picotees that distinguish many of the stunning specimens. Gold tones are popular, appearing in 'Horizon Monarch', 'Invitation', and 'Capistrano'.

A fairly recent feature, the Ramsey Rock Garden boasts intriguing dwarf specimens of conifers, rhododendrons, and companion plants. A refreshing Meditation Garden is sited adjacent to a pond. The garden's large outcroppings of rocks intermingle with ferns, primulas, and Japanese, Siberian, and German bearded iris.

At Meerkerk Gardens, late March is full with the blooms of early rhododendrons, magnolia trees, dwarf iris, and narcissus. A show of more than 100,000 bulbs lights up the surroundings in spring before the garden's peak bloom time, with its brilliant display of magnolias, cherries, rhododendrons, azaleas, and daffodils.

A new Blue Bell Wood is located in the Meerkerk's original Secret Garden. A gift of the Greenbank Garden Club, it celebrates the 25th anniversary of the Gardens.

❀ **Admission:** Fee.

Garden open: Daily 9:00 A.M. to 4:00 P.M. Call to confirm hours.

Further information: Visit the Web site for information on special events or to view a map. Call for details if you wish to arrange a group tour. Restrooms are available March through October. The gardens are partially wheelchair accessible via the main walking loop.

Directions: Meerkerk Gardens are on Whidbey Island, south of Greenbank, at Highway 525 and Resort Road; about an hour-and-a-half drive north of Seattle (including a twenty-minute ferry crossing). Take the Mukilteo Ferry to Clinton; from Clinton, take Highway 525 north approximately 15 miles, turn right onto Resort Road, and left onto Meerkerk Lane (signs are posted).

6. Hummingbird Farm Nursery and Gardens

2319 Zylstra Road, **Oak Harbor,**
WA 98277; (360) 679–5044;
www.hummingbirdfarmnursery.com

*H*UMMINGBIRD FARM boasts exceedingly photogenic fences and arbors of a distinctive periwinkle blue hue. You may have serendipitously viewed images of the establishment's delightful display gardens—including a cottage garden and moon garden—in magazines or on television gardening shows that feature numerous plants found in the nursery's inventory.

Visit the nursery, where you will discover a large selection of new and unusual varieties of perennials, herbs, annuals, shrubs, ornamental grasses, and roses. Then take a stroll through the enchanting gardens, which reveal the mature fullness and height of plantings now more than ten years old. In midsummer, hollyhocks and roses lend old-fashioned grace to beds and borders teeming with fragrant blooming herbs and perennials. As new plants are introduced, the gardens evolve, so a subsequent visit may yield exciting new plants to pique your interest. You'll see especially lavish floral displays in June and July. The ample, textural foliage and handsome forms of bountiful grasses, shrubs, and trees encircling the garden areas provide year-round interest.

Hummingbird Farm also features a popular garden shop stocked with handcrafted rustic furniture and home- and garden-themed gifts. Hummingbird feeders are a specialty item, along with unique items representative of Whidbey Island and the region.

❀ **Admission:** Free.

Garden open: Wednesday through Sunday 10:00 A.M. to 6:00 P.M. and open by appointment. Closings can occur from time to time, so it's best to call before you visit.

Further information: Check the Web site's calendar page for up-to-date details, to view a map, or to contact proprietors Lee and Lori Spear via e-mail. Wheelchair accessibility is limited.

Directions: Located on the north end of Whidbey Island, between Coupeville and Oak Harbor, Hummingbird Farm is about two hours from Seattle by either the Mukilteo–Clinton Ferry or the Deception Pass Bridge. Detailed directions are found on the Web site.

Seattle and East King County
Gardenwalks

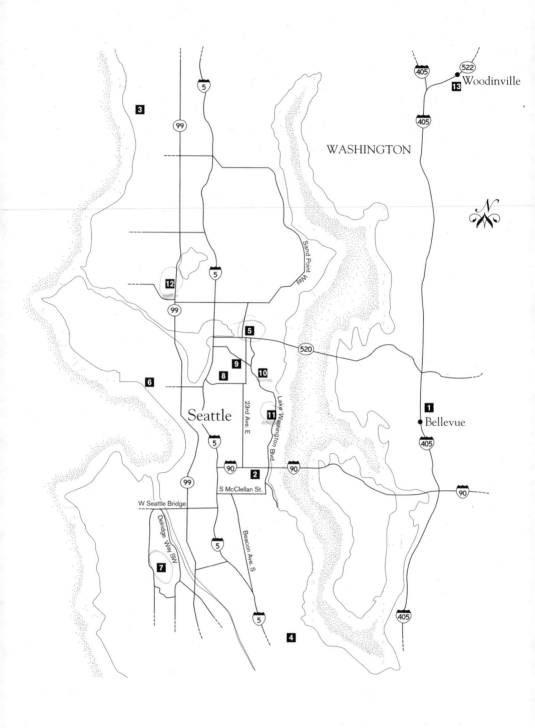

3

522

405

13 Woodinville

WASHINGTON

405

99

5

Sand Point Way

5

12

99

5

520

5

9

10

8

6

Seattle

23rd Ave E

Lake Washington Blvd

1

Bellevue

11

5

405

90

2

90

90

99

S McClellan St.

W Seattle Bridge

Delridge Way SW

5

Beacon Ave. S

7

5

405

4

1. Bellevue: Bellevue Botanical Garden
2. Seattle: Bradner Gardens Park
3. Seattle: Dunn Gardens
4. Seattle: Kubota Garden
5. Seattle: Medicinal Herb Garden, University of Washington
6. Seattle: Parsons Garden
7. Seattle: Seattle Chinese Garden (Xi Hua Yuan) at South Seattle Community College
8. Seattle: Volunteer Park
9. Seattle: Volunteer Park Conservatory
10. Seattle: Washington Park Arboretum
11. Seattle: Washington Park Arboretum's Japanese Garden
12. Seattle: Woodland Park Rose Garden
13. Woodinville: Molbak's Nursery

1. Bellevue Botanical Garden

12001 Main Street, **Bellevue,** WA 98005; (425) 452–2750;
www.bellevuebotanical.org

$\mathcal{B}$Y VIRTUE of its matchless perennial borders, the Bellevue Botanical Garden attracts eager garden travelers much like a beehive brimming with honey draws bears. Established in 1992 through the initiative and creative energy of members affiliated with the Northwest Perennial Alliance, plus the Bellevue Parks and Community Services Department, the garden quickly achieved national prominence. Operated today by the parks department in partnership with the Botanical Garden Society, the Bellevue Botanical Garden continues to prosper and grow in scope.

The garden occupies a thirty-six-acre segment of Wilburton Hill Park. Over time the amazingly lush, stunningly designed borders developed along with a number of prominent gardens and special features. A lovely water element—a rill—distinguishes the appealing entry plaza and visitor center. The flow of water through the rill's narrow channel effectively and appealingly draws attention to the garden's entryway. Wrapping around the north and west side of the center, the Waterwise Garden inspires home gardeners with its exhibition of handsome, drought-tolerant specimens meant to bring beauty to every season.

Installed in 1996, the visually dramatic Alpine Rock Garden features a tiered arrangement, highlighted by rugged basalt outcrops. The agreeably open setting, with its assured hardscaping, provides a perfect haven for a rock garden and alpine plants. Take a quiet interlude and visit the Yao Japanese Garden, which presents

The Bellevue Look

If you're hoping to locate horticultural rarieties like the out-standing plants established at Bellevue Botanical Garden, refer to the nursery write-ups elsewhere in this book, including Heronswood and Cultus Bay; Cistus and Joy Creek in the Port-land area; and Gossler Farms in Springfield.

Pacific Northwest and Asian plants in a blend of contemporary and traditional Asian landscape design.

Other collections of flora emphasize fuchsias and ground covers, while special changing displays highlight dahlias, flowering annuals, and hardy ferns. You'll have wonderful opportunities for contemplative nature walks along the garden's Loop Trail, which winds gracefully through the botanical reserve's woodlands, wet-lands, and meadows.

During a midsummer sojourn to the Bellevue Botanical Gar-den, my great expectations were exceeded. Although I had heard glowing reviews of the garden's famed perennial borders, I was unprepared for their spectacular impact. I paused to marvel at the exceptional collection of hydrangeas in the Shade Border and then proceeded to explore the 17,000-square-foot area of sunny plantings. The diversity of plants found in these voluminous borders is tes-tament to the widespread interest in perennial gardening, and the borders provide undeniable evidence of the wealth of exciting new plants that nurseries are propagating. What an exciting challenge they present to a gardener who is interested in expanding the reper-toire of plant material at home. In the Main Border look for keenly arranged color groupings that pleasingly jostle the senses. Cerise with chartreuse, for one, surprises both connoisseurs and the average onlooker.

It's impossible to miss the Hot Border! Sizzling in July with bright reds, oranges, and brilliant yellows, the showy exhibition here includes daylilies, branching floriferous crocosmia, red-hot pokers, and the like. You can penetrate the interior of this perennial border by following the hazelnut path, where you'll be enveloped by the intoxicating mix of shrubs, perennials, bulbs, vines, annuals, and ornamental grasses. This area is bound to generate a wish list of plants that gardeners want to grow in their own landscapes.

Plan enough time to savor the borders' tapestry of horticultural rarities—many of which boast sublime variegation, dazzling colors, or lavish bloom. You won't be disappointed.

✿ **Admission:** Free.

Garden open: Daily, including holidays, from dawn to dusk. The visitor center is open 9:00 A.M. to 4:00 P.M.

Further information: Special events are listed on the Web site, along with a "seasonal palette" to whet your appetite before visiting. Call or check the Web site for times for guided tours, generally offered on Saturday and Sunday from April through October. Free group tours are available if arranged in advance; call or look on the Web site for tour information. The garden is partially ADA accessible; most major pathways are wheelchair accessible, but some smaller pathways are not.

Directions: Bellevue is located just east of Seattle across Lake Washington. If you avoid rush-hour traffic, the drive to Bellevue should take twenty minutes or so. You'll find driving directions, bus routes, and a map on the Bellevue Botanical Garden Web site.

2. Bradner Gardens Park

Twenty-ninth Avenue South and South Grand Street,
Seattle, WA; (206) 684–4075 (Seattle Parks and Recreation);
www.cityofseattle.net/parks

*A*N INTRIGUING entrance arbor serves as a portal to this new 1.6-acre park in the Mount Baker neighborhood. In addition to the arbor, a footbridge and shade garden trellis represent design and construction projects undertaken by architecture students affiliated with the University of Washington's Howard S. Wright Design/Build Studio.

The park's no-pesticides policy, together with a commitment to sustainable gardening practices, informs visitors that this collaborative venture between the surrounding Seattle community and a host of volunteer organizations is on the right track.

Here you'll discover myriad ornamental gardens, including a master gardener border where the plantings are designed to attract butterflies and hummingbirds. Fragrance, sensory, shade, and xeriscape themes also appear, along with an arrangement of Northwest natives and another with winter interest in mind.

Follow the curving pathways and you'll come upon demonstration areas encompassing an educational display about growing food crops (under the auspices of Seattle Tilth) and a parade of ornamental street trees that do well in small spaces.

The charming footbridge leads to a pavilion situated in a central section of the parkland. In this inviting environment many surprising elements—in the form of artful objects—emerge as garden travelers meander from place to place. Look for lovely mosaics, unique benches, and whimsical scarecrows, as well as practical devices like a vintage windmill, enlivening the park's creative atmosphere.

✿ **Admission:** Free.

Garden open: Daily 4:30 A.M. to 11:30 P.M.

Further information: Check the Web site for news of special events. Paths throughout the park and bathroom facilities are ADA accessible.

Directions: Located in southeast Seattle's Mount Baker neighborhood. You'll find directions to the park by bus or by car on the Web site.

3. Dunn Gardens

E. B. Dunn Historic Garden Trust, P.O. Box 77126, **Seattle,** WA 98177; (206) 362-0933; www.dunngardens.org

*I*N 1914 Arthur Dunn acquired a ten-acre parcel of land in what was to become Seattle's Broadview neighborhood. The wooded site of second-growth Douglas firs and expansive, open areas offered breathtaking vistas of Puget Sound and the Olympic Mountains.

Acclaimed for their landscape design work, the Olmsted Brothers were contacted by Dunn the following year with a request that they create the garden layout for the family's summer home. The Dunns' original country retreat was designed by architect Charles Gould in a shingled Arts and Crafts style; however, it was taken down and another house was built at a later date.

Currently a lyrical naturalism distinguishes the Dunn Gardens' landscaping. Thanks to garden restoration work, you will experience impressions akin to what one would have enjoyed when the Olmsted plan was first unveiled so many years ago.

Visitors may anticipate strolling the 8.2-acre gardens, located under a canopy of native firs and introduced hardwoods and enhanced by meadowlike lawns. Here you will bask in the magic of the Olmsted transformation of the site's terrain, with its gentle slope toward the Puget Sound.

A comprehensive circulation pattern encompasses the garden. The arrangement includes curving pathways that trace the existing topography and, at the same time, delineate inviting walks that lead to various garden areas, quiet corners, and a drive that follows a ravine on the property's southern edge.

The Olmsteds set the garden so that the grades are fairly gentle in most instances. The careful placement of paths allows visitors to appreciate the heart of this wonderful garden and its lovely views without having to travel through the full space. If you are unable to go down one path to get into a part of the garden, for instance, there will be another place where you can look into the same area from above.

Outstanding plants are too numerous to mention, but whenever you visit, expect to find dazzling displays of rarities as you explore the garden's rooms and green swaths of lawn.

In early spring the mesmerizing fawn lily (*Erythronium revolutum* and *E. oreganum*) appears in combination with camellias, snowdrops, daffodils, and hellebores. In the Upper Ravine Glade, the Barbara Leede Bayley Memorial Walk, the Pond Garden, and other sequestered spots, look for conspicuous displays of trillium. Some ten varieties of this most magical of springtime flowers bolster the landscape.

As spring progresses, wood anemones emerge, in association with maidenhair ferns and giant Himalayan lilies (*Cardiocrinum giganteum*). Stunning specimens such as *Camellia japonica* 'Auburn White', with its glowing blooms, can be found in the curators' garden, where it is shaped to grow in a single trunk.

Equally as lovely, *Rhododendron calophytum* is a showy species growing at the entrance to Ed Dunn's Woodland Garden. One of Arthur Dunn's sons, Edward gardened here for decades, developing an environment befitting the spirit and intention of the Olmsted Brothers' design.

Since rising to prominence with their design of the Bellevue Botanical Gardens Perennial Border, Glenn Withey and Charles Price, the Dunn Gardens' curators, are widely celebrated and in demand as speakers and designers.

Working within the exceptional framework of the Dunn Gardens, Withey Price (as they are known) have renovated Ed Dunn's mixed perennial border and worked to restore the understory plantings in the spirit of the original Olmsted design, achieving a visual excitement melded with a corresponding refinement.

To celebrate summer in the curators' garden, they create stunning container plantings filled with boldly contrasting colors and textural foliage. In the hands of these inspired plantsmen, the presence of a full-bodied terra-cotta vessel commands attention. Overflowing with tender beauties, an arrangement might include the patterned leaves of a pelargonium playing off burnt-orange coleus and the zesty coral-pink trailing blooms of a calibrachoa. The elongated blades of a choice *Cordyline* specimen counterbalance the softened aspect of the overall form.

Japanese anemones can be counted on for a superb performance in the autumn, complementing hardy *Cyclamen hederifolium* blooming through the fall in many areas of the garden. The asters, dahlias, *Phygelius*, and phlox in Ed's Perennial Border give color well into autumn. Along the woodland walk on the northern border of the property, hydrangeas put on a sumptuous show.

As the Olmsteds had accommodated Arthur Dunn's request to incorporate the hardwood trees that he loved as a child in New York, Ed Dunn, who loved nut trees, extended that distinctive mix of deciduous trees and conifers by planting a number of Asian chestnuts to grace the southeast woodland area of the garden.

Marking a splendid time in the Dunn Gardens, the fall season strikes a chord among visitors, as these trees increase the impact of the surroundings. Plan to visit the Dunn Gardens at this time of year, and you'll enjoy the turning maple leaves together with a fiery assemblage composed of tulip tree, crab apple and Persian ironwood (*Parrotia persica*), among others.

✿ **Admission:** Fee.

Garden open: By appointment only April through July and September through October; call well in advance to arrange a visit. The gardens are closed in August.

Further information: Check the Web site's event calendar to learn about special lectures and tour details. The gardens are barrier free and partially wheelchair accessible. The restroom, most of the trails, and the walks are negotiable with a wheelchair. Benches are placed in many areas that allow for short rests; there are easy ways to then reconnect with a tour.

Victoria Clipper

If your Seattle-area journey finds you short on time, you can still plan a convenient visit to Vancouver Island on the Victoria Clipper. Passengers board the clipper at Pier 69 in downtown Seattle and disembark the ship at Victoria's Inner Harbour. Plan ahead and you might choose a special-interest getaway from Clipper Vacations; some include bus or rail travel. On offer, for instance, are day trips to the Sequim Lavender Festival or an overnight sojourn to the city of Vancouver. To book your adventure online, log on to www.clippervacations.com. Or call toll-free (800) 888–2535 for information. While in Seattle, call (206) 448–5000; from Victoria, British Columbia, call (250) 382–8100.

Directions: The Dunn Gardens are 10 miles north of downtown Seattle, south of the Highlands area. Directions are provided on confirmation of a reservation.

4. Kubota Garden

Renton Avenue South at Fifty-fifth Avenue South,
Seattle, WA (mailing address: Kubota Garden Foundation,
P.O. Box 78338, Seattle, WA 98178); (206) 684-4584;
www.kubota.org

*T*HE TWENTY-ACRE Kubota Garden was begun in 1927 by Fujitaro Kubota. A self-taught gardener and Japanese emigrant, Kubota established a thriving landscaping business in the Seattle area and designed the extensive gardens surrounding his own home and business. He left behind a significant horticultural legacy that includes designing the Japanese Garden at the Bloedel Reserve on Bainbridge Island and another at Seattle University.

Now a historical landmark, the Kubota Garden evolved over decades as Kubota installed water features, planted excellent tree specimens, and creatively arranged stone to further proclaim the beauty of the landscape.

The cruel internment of the Kubota family in the 1940s resulted in the garden's being abandoned for four years. When the war ended, the family returned to their land, and Kubota and his two sons resumed operation of their company. They proceeded to cultivate pine trees—their specialty. If you consult the garden's self-guided tour map, you'll note an area where outstanding examples of Japanese black and red pines coexist, symbolizing male and female energy.

The Kubota Garden was acquired by the city of Seattle from the Kubota family in 1987. Today the secluded setting is a wonderful respite from the city's more crowded tourist attractions. Garden features include the Necklace of Ponds with Heart Bridge, the Bamboo Grove planted with yellow and black groove bamboo, and the Mountainside with its waterfall, reflection pools, and carved stones.

On a visit here you'll have an opportunity to see many rare and beautiful plants, including the bamboo *Phyllostachys nigra* 'Meguro-chiku'. The Meeting Lawn presents a splendid vignette composed of two unusually expressive trees—a 32-foot-long weeping blue Atlas cedar juxtaposed with a 37-foot-high weeping Norway spruce.

Within the overall plan of the Kubota Garden, an area known as the Japanese Garden traces its roots to the 1930s. This serene space is designed in the tradition of Japan's best-known garden style.

Tom Kubota, son of Fujitaro, remained committed to the garden's future. His vision, together with the support of the city parks department, the Kubota Garden Foundation, and generous donations by volunteers, led to a groundbreaking ceremony for the Tom Kubota Stroll Garden in the summer of 1999. The lovely new garden, situated near Renton Avenue South, was inaugurated in the spring of 2000. Its meandering pathways are punctuated by the curving profile and vivid red hue of a painted footbridge. According to a foundation volunteer, the garden enhances a less usable area of the garden and will allow less energetic visitors to enjoy its beauty and tranquillity.

✿ **Admission:** Free.

Garden open: Daily during daylight hours.

Further information: Detailed self-guided maps of the garden are available at the information kiosk. Look for a schedule of events on the Web site, including free public tours. Individual garden visitors are welcome anytime. To schedule a guided tour for eight or more visitors, contact the Kubota Garden Foundation at (206) 725–5060. Accessibility for walkers and wheelchairs is limited.

Directions: Kubota Garden is located in the Rainier Beach neighborhood of South Seattle. You'll find detailed directions and a map on the Web site.

5. Medicinal Herb Garden, University of Washington

South-central area of campus, opposite the Botany Greenhouse, off Stevens Way, **Seattle,** WA (mailing address: University of Washington, Box 351800, Seattle, WA 98195-1500); (206) 543-1126; http://nnlm.gov/pnr/uwmhg

*E*XTENSIVE paths flow through the University of Washington's beautiful, densely wooded campus. Obtain a map of the campus beforehand, or ask the gatekeeper for directions, and you'll soon discover the series of outdoor rooms of the Medicinal Herb Garden affiliated with the university's botany department.

Of particular interest to herbalists and botanists, the medical community, and garden lovers are the garden's 600 species of beneficial plants. Approximately two-thirds are represented in a fine collection of shrubs and trees that border the Medicinal Herb Garden's adjacent arrangement of spaces. The remaining species are an interesting assortment of familiar and unusual plants that grow in a framework of formal raised beds emphasized by wooden frames.

The plants are sited in islands of sun or, in the case of shade-loving species, shielded by towering trees. Throughout the Medicinal Herb Garden, precise labels identify all the specimens and enlighten visitors about the collection in general. Look, for example, for the rare camphor tree (*Cinnamomum camphorum*).

Dating from 1911, the Medicinal Herb Garden reaches peak bloom in May and June but is worthy of a visit during each and every month of the year. Gigantic castor bean (an annual in Seattle's climate) and masses of joe-pye weed presented a dazzling exhibition on the summery day I last visited. Early in the year, look among a host of agreeable plants for the attractive foliage of winter-blooming hellebores. At this time you'll also see the interesting branching forms of witch hazels decorated with delicate clusters of bright flowers.

Northwest Flower & Garden Show

For some two decades, Seattle's Northwest Flower & Garden Show has presented tantalizing garden exhibits on its five acres. The Northwest region's top-notch exhibition draws garden lovers from near and far to revel in beautifully produced show gardens and see the wares of a plethora of retail exhibitors catering to every imaginable gardening niche.

An exceptional yearly event held during February, the Northwest Flower & Garden Show presents an international roster of trend-setting designers and horticultural visionaries who offer ongoing garden talks. Audiences are entertained and motivated by a wide range of topics, from container gardening and craft projects to selecting and designing with bulbs, grasses, and perennials. These seminars offer a wealth of inventive possibilities and suggestions on how to transform the garden design at home into a landscape of uncommon beauty. You can look forward to the promise of a satisfying horticultural adventure.

The show is held at the Washington State Convention Center, located at Seventh Avenue and Pike Street, just off Interstate 5 in downtown Seattle. Direct your Internet browser to www.gardenshow.com for additional location information, directions, descriptions of displays, a schedule of seminars, and all the latest news. Or call the hotline at (800) 229-6311 for dates and times (206-789-5333 in the Seattle area).

Thanks to its wide-ranging educational displays of beneficial plants, the Medicinal Herb Garden at the University of Washington holds an important place in the long-standing tradition of using herbs for health purposes.

❀ **Admission:** Free.

Garden open: Daily during daylight hours.

Further information: The Web site contains a trove of botanical information and a map of the garden. Contact the Medicinal Herb Garden c/o the Biology Department, University of Washington, at the mailing address listed above. The garden's walkways are wheelchair accessible.

Directions: The garden is on the campus of the University of Washington in Seattle. Northeast Forty-fifth Street runs along the university's northern boundary, Union Bay borders the eastern periphery of the campus, and Portage Bay borders the southwestern edge.

6. Parsons Garden

Seventh Avenue West and West Highland Drive, **Seattle,** WA 98119; (206) 684–4075 (Seattle Parks and Recreation); www.cityofseattle.net/parks

*D*ESIGNATED a landmark by Seattle's Landmarks Preservation Board, the Parsons Garden was once the personal garden of Mr. and Mrs. Reginald H. Parsons. In 1956 the couple's children gave the garden to the citizens of Seattle, and now garden travelers can enjoy its very special ambience.

A popular site for weddings, Parsons Garden is a delightful, small-scale gem of a landscape. Its lush lawn area, circular path, and flowing borders come alive with springtime flowering displays and offer a perfect place to unwind should your Seattle sojourn take you to Seattle's Queen Anne neighborhood.

❀ **Admission:** Free.

Garden open: Daily 4:00 A.M. to 11:30 P.M.

Further information: The garden is partially wheelchair accessible.

Directions: The garden is located immediately west of 618 West Highland Drive, on the southwest crest of Seattle's Queen Anne Hill. Detailed directions are on the Web site.

7. Seattle Chinese Garden (Xi Hua Yuan) at South Seattle Community College

6000 Sixteenth Avenue SW (north entry), **Seattle,** WA 98106-1499; (206) 282–8040; www.seattle-chinese-garden.org

*I*N THE SPRING of 1999, a team of Chinese craftsmen—two stone carvers, two carpenters, a stonemason, a painter, a landscape architect, and an engineer—arrived in Seattle to assemble the Song Mei Pavilion, a small open-air structure with a flared roof. It is surrounded by a 10,000-square-foot demonstration garden displaying rare flora from China.

Song Mei will serve as a demonstration garden while the Seattle Chinese Garden Society—which is supported by business, civic, and educational groups—raises funds to begin major construction of a six-acre classical Chinese garden.

The Seattle Chinese Garden Society's lofty goal is to build a garden based upon a 2,000-year-old tradition. Highlighted by ponds, rock features, paths, and framed views, the parklike Sichuan/Chongqing-style garden promises to introduce visitors to a rare aesthetic beauty as well as to the symbolism inherent in classical Chinese gardens. Views of Seattle's downtown area, the Olympic and Cascade Mountains, and Elliott Bay add drama to the site of the Seattle Chinese Garden. When completed, the garden will convey the principle of a vast universe while expressing culturally significant artistic, philosophical, and horticultural attributes.

❀ **Admission:** Free.

Garden open: Daily dawn to dusk; closed holidays.

Further information: Check the Web site for project updates and to learn about special festivals and events taking place at the Seattle Chinese Garden. Free guided tours are offered; call for details or visit the Web site for dates and times. Public tours last approximately an hour and a half; no reservation is necessary. Groups can call the Seattle Chinese Garden Society office at (206) 282–8040 to arrange a group tour; or write to 500 Union Street, Suite 1045, Seattle, WA 98101. Crushed granite pathways provide wheelchair accessibility.

Directions: The garden is in West Seattle, off the West Seattle Freeway from either Interstate 5 or Highway 99. Detailed driving directions are found on the Web site, where you can also download a map.

8. Volunteer Park

1247 Fifteenth Avenue East, **Seattle,** WA 98112; (206) 684–4555; www.cityofseattle.net/parks

*V*OLUNTEER PARK is a distinctive green space within Seattle's extensive system of parks. Designed by the Olmsted Brothers, landscape architects and sons of Frederick Law Olmsted, the forty-eight-acre park is well known for its water tower, which provides a panoramic view of the city and beyond. You'll find the water tower located at the south entrance to the park.

Most recently the nonprofit Seattle Parks Foundation helped raise funding to restore the park's historic Lily Ponds. Included in the original Olmsted Brothers plan, the ponds now feature shade-tolerant varieties of lovely water lilies.

❈ **Admission:** Free.

Garden open: Daily 6:00 A.M. to 11:00 P.M.

Further information: Many pathways in the park are paved and wheelchair accessible.

Directions: The park is located in the heart of Seattle, east of Lake Union, in the Capitol Hill neighborhood. Look on the Web site for public transportation information and for detailed driving directions.

9. Volunteer Park Conservatory

1400 East Galer Street, **Seattle,** WA 98112; (206) 684–4743; www.cityofseattle.net/parks

A STUNNING Victorian-style glass conservatory located at the north end of this parkland is not to be missed! Dating from 1914 when the conservatory opened to the public, the elegant, aesthetic building captivates garden travelers. Its two opposing wings hold wonderful collections of bromeliads at one end and cacti and succulents at the other.

As you enter the conservatory, the Palm House displays such fine plants as orchids, anthuriums from Hawaii, crotons from tropical climes, and exuberant ginger plants. Reaching high into the dome of the building, a towering fiddleleaf fig tree is a particularly impressive sight.

In the Seasonal Display House, changing plant exhibitions inaugurate spring, summer, and fall themes. Bulbs and lilies are highlights all throughout springtime, while begonias light up the summer months. Fragrant gardenias and colorful chrysanthemums bring a special beauty to the fall. End-of-the-year holidays are celebrated with a show of poinsettias, of course, guaranteed to brighten any span of gray days.

Prepare to be delighted by arrays of exotic looking euphorbia species, oddly hairy *Notocactus*, the ferociously handsome blue cycad, and *Mammillaria* with bright red thorns taking up residence in the arid conditions of the Cactus House. When many of the succulents like prickly pears (*Opuntia* sp.) and their allies burst into flower, the show becomes still more spectacular. The ornamental blooms beam brightly in shades from amber gold to saffron, burnt crimson, magenta, and amethyst.

You'll discover exactingly cared for horticultural specimens appearing in the Fern House. Compelling species of cycads consort with alluring angel's trumpet (*Brugmansia*) and enthralling bird of paradise.

❀ **Admission:** Free.

Garden open: Daily, including holidays, 10:00 A.M. to 7:00 P.M. from Memorial Day through Labor Day; 10:00 A.M. to 4:00 P.M. at other times of the year.

Further information: Call the Friends of the Conservatory at (206) 322–4112 for details on special guided tours, plant sales, and special events; or visit the Web site. Wheelchair accessibility is good overall, except for a couple of narrow doorways.

Directions: Volunteer Park is in the city's Capitol Hill neighborhood, off the Seattle Freeway, east of Lake Union. You'll find detailed directions for arriving by bus or by car on the Web site.

10. Washington Park Arboretum

Graham Visitors Center, 2300 Arboretum Drive East,
Seattle, WA 98112; (206) 543–8800, (206) 684–4075
(Seattle Parks and Recreation); www.depts.washington.edu/wpa

*D*ESIGNED BY the renowned Olmsted Brothers, scions of Frederick Law Olmsted, the city of Seattle's fine boulevard plan and park system suggest plenty of reasons to explore neighborhoods throughout town. The well-endowed Washington Park Arboretum and tranquil landscape of the Japanese Garden play a prominent role among Seattle's treasure trove of parkland settings.

In a region where gardening activities are a significant pastime for so many area residents, the Washington Park Arboretum is maintained by the energetic members of the Arboretum Foundation, a host of volunteers, the staff affiliated with the Seattle Parks and Recreation Department, and the University of Washington in association with the Center for Urban Horticulture.

Seattle's excellent arboretum deserves a visit (or two or three) whenever you find yourself in the city. More than 4,600 different types of woody plants are cultivated on the arboretum's 230-acre grounds. Among the diverse species, are important collections of rhododendron, cherry, pine, Japanese maple, and holly. Every month offers something unique to engage the interest of garden lovers. Pick up a trail map at the Graham Visitors Center and stroll over to the Azalea Way. In April this three-quarter-acre area features a parade of flowering dogwoods, cherries, and of course azaleas. The beautiful display here promises to brighten a damp or dreary springtime mood with a sensory assault of the highest order. When bathed in dappled sunlight, this floral arena glistens.

Gorgeous magnolias and lush conifers harbor large-leaved rhododendrons in an area known as Loderi Valley. The collection of "rhodies" blooms from February into June, while the peak exhibition of magnolias spans March through May. The delightful Joseph A. Witt Winter Garden is especially splendid from November through March. For your tour of the Arboretum Self-Guided Waterfront Trail, look for a special pamphlet distinguished by a lovely line drawing on its cover. As the trail meanders over marshlands and a bridge, you'll have up close and personal views of Marsh Island and Foster Island, with all the flora and fauna that coexist in a marshland environment. The delightful booklet illustrates plants and creatures found along the way and describes the evolution of the area's landmass and waterways.

On a midsummer tour of Seattle and the arboretum, I happened upon an extraordinary horticultural ode to color installed in a planting area dubbed the Arboretum Signature Bed. An exciting project, the Signature Bed changes each year when a select group of volunteers takes charge of designing, establishing, and maintaining a special theme planting intended for year-round interest. The "Bold & Beautiful" project, which was thriving during my late July visit, was true to its name. It completely charmed me. On view from October through September of the following year, this particular Signature Bed was presented by the Myrtle DeFreil Unit 16 of the Arboretum Foundation, featuring a dynamite design by Richard W. Hartlage, author of *Bold Visions for the Garden* and former director and curator of the Miller Botanical Garden. The plantings conveyed high drama through the use of plant selections characterized by strong architectural forms, arresting textural contrasts, and intense colors. The purples, reds, and yellows of the sumptuous foliage and flowers expressed a joyous energy that was a pleasure to observe.

An A to Z of unusual species and cultivars—*Abutilons* to *Zantedeschias*—starred in the Bold & Beautiful extravaganza which was distinguished by fiery, tropical elements that continue to gain popularity among gardening zealots. *Ensete ventricosum* 'Maurellii', with its huge leaves, towered over coveys of flamboyant cannas, excessive coleus specimens (with wonderful monikers like 'Inky Fingers', 'Kiwi Fern', and 'Purple Emperor'), lush fuchsias, and the striking swords of *Phormium tenax* 'Atrosanguineum'.

Based upon the Signature Bed's scintillating exhibition during that special July day, I can only imagine the beauty of its earlier permutation in winter and spring seasons. Needless to say, I can't wait to return to investigate the changing designs and witness the creative outpouring of planting ideas in years to come.

In addition, a recently crafted master plan for the arboretum promises exciting changes to take place in the coming years. Dozens of renovated and new plant exhibits are in planning stage, along with refreshed trails for pedestrians and bicyclists. The Graham Visitors Center will be expanded and refurbished, while concentrated activity at the Japanese Garden (see the gardenwalk entry that follows) has already resulted in a renovation that made it ADA compliant.

❀ **Admission:** Free.

Garden open: Daily dawn to dusk. The Graham Visitors Center and Gift Shop is open daily 10:00 A.M. to 4:00 P.M.

Further information: The gates on the north and south end of Arboretum Drive East are closed during nonopen hours. Check the Web site for an up-to-date schedule of free guided tours beginning at the Graham

Visitors Center. Contact the Arboretum Foundation at (206) 325–4510 or www.wparboretum.org for news of special events. The arboretum is partially wheelchair accessible.

Directions: The arboretum is in Central Seattle, east of downtown and south of the University of Washington, on the shores of Lake Washington. Check the Web site for a map, detailed driving directions, and public transit information.

11. Washington Park Arboretum's Japanese Garden

1075 Lake Washington Boulevard East, **Seattle,** WA; (206) 684–4725; www.cityofseattle.net/parks

*A*TTENTION to detail is characteristic of the authentic style you'll enjoy when touring Seattle's Japanese Garden. An anecdote of an early phase of the garden's history serves to sum up the type of efforts involved in creating a garden that would faithfully encompass ancient traditions of Japanese garden design. Juki Iida, the garden's primary designer, initially worked with a number of other designers to produce pages of plans documenting the three-and-a-half-acre garden's layout. Arriving in the United States from Japan, Iida proceeded to choose 500 massive boulders from their natural mountainous environment, and he then personally supervised the placing of the formidable architectural forms that were so essential to the philosophical and artistic underpinnings of the landscaping. Such uncompromising efforts led to the beauty of this garden.

On your self-guided tour of the Japanese Garden, pass through the South Gate and follow along the east path past the waterfall. In the exemplary Tea Garden, featuring a Shoseian teahouse structure, you'll sense the reflective atmosphere associated with the tradition of the tea ceremony. On entering the tea garden, visitors pass into a consecrated realm where the world is left behind. Inside the garden's discrete setting, a bamboo fence delineates two areas: an outer area where guests convene, and an inner area designed to give pause for ritual purification before entering the teahouse. An arbor indicates the garden's waiting area, while the inner section is distinguished by a stone basin for washing.

Walking the Japanese Garden's paths, you'll find a host of lovely features to contemplate. Water elements abound; they are crucial to the beauty and symbolism of Japanese gardens. Here are the waterfall's soothing intonations and streams that merge to form the lake. Note the turtle island rising above the lake's glassy surface, with the restrained, sculpturelike arrangement of three Japanese red pines. And on Nakajima Island, which can be reached by either earthen or plank bridge, observe pine trees representing cranes, the symbols of long life.

Viewing the pleasing asymmetry of the lake's outline, the unequal groupings of trees, or the placement of outcroppings, you'll discover that what at first appears to be randomness can serve, when studied, to interpret essential ideals of balance and harmony. The garden's shapes and forms, and its arrangements of plants, hardscaping, and ornamentation, embody deliberate decisions that artfully imply mountains, forests, rivers, and plateaus of the natural world.

At the northern reaches of the garden, a handsome arbor with a roof of bamboo trelliswork stands just at the point of the lake's outlet. A mature wisteria supported by the arbor grows forth from a timeworn trunk, suggesting venerable old age. Here again you can reflect on how such dissimilarities contribute to the meditative qualities of this beautiful Japanese Garden.

❀ **Admission:** Fee.

    Garden open: Tuesday through Sunday at 10:00 A.M.; closing hours vary. The garden may close for special events. Call for hours before visiting.

    Further information: A recent renovation greatly improved wheelchair access; also, several accessible vantage points allow for observation of the garden.

Directions: The Japanese Garden is on Lake Washington Boulevard East, north of East Madison Street and south of the arboretum's visitor center; refer to the directions for the Washington Park Arboretum. Check the Web site for detailed directions.

12. Woodland Park Rose Garden

700 North Fiftieth Street at Fremont Avenue North,
Seattle, WA 98103; (206) 684-4863; www.cityofseattle.net/parks

*R*OSES THRIVE in Seattle's moderate climate and moist conditions. Under the auspices of the Seattle Parks and Recreation Department and the Woodland Park Zoo, a fine showcase for these gorgeous blooms is maintained at the Woodland Park Rose Garden. Devoted to the cultivation and exhibition of roses, the two-and-a-half-acre rose garden opened in 1924. Currently 260 varieties of roses are featured, with some 5,000 rosebushes adorning the lovely landscaped grounds.

Grass pathways weave through the Woodland Park Rose Garden's appealing layout, ornamented by a handsome bas-relief sculpture designed by Alice Carr, a reflecting pool, and a gazebo. In addition to lavish displays of roses, the garden features a number of rare oriental cypress trees (*Chamaecyparis pisifera* 'Squarrosa'). Known commonly as moss cypress or moss falsecypress, the geometrically arranged trees lend a handsome structure to the garden plan. Pruned in outstanding sculptural topiary forms that accentuate the trees' grayish-blue, needlelike foliage, the beautiful arboreal specimens contribute elements of fantasy to the setting.

One of the United States' twenty-four All-America Rose Selections Test Gardens is located within the boundaries of the Woodland Park Rose Garden. You'll be able to peek at the new varieties being considered by growers while enjoying a wide range of tried-and-true shrub roses, hybrid teas, and climbers praised for their vigor and radiance.

You may want to keep in mind that peak bloom time for the garden is late June through the end of August. Note, however, that climbing roses start blooming in April, and all the roses continue to bloom until the end of October.

❀ **Admission:** Free.

Garden open: Daily 4:00 A.M. to 11:30 P.M.

Further information: Call the Woodland Park Zoo information line at (206) 684–4040 or contact the rose garden directly at the number above. Contact the Seattle Parks and Recreation Department at (206) 684–4075 for general information. Individual garden visitors are always welcome. Phone for details on tours for groups of ten or more; two weeks' notice is required (tours are held weekdays between 7:00 A.M. and 3:30 P.M.). No fee is charged for the tours, but donations are encouraged. The terrain is flat with unpaved paths. Grass pathways and some crushed granite walkways accommodate wheelchairs.

Directions: The rose garden is adjacent to the Woodland Park Zoo, in the Greenwood/Phinney/Fremont/Wallingford neighborhood of Seattle. Log on to www.zoo.org for public transit information, driving directions, or a map.

13. Molbak's Nursery

13625 Northeast 175th Street, **Woodinville**, WA 98072; (425) 483–5000; www.molbaks.com

*A*T THE family-owned Molbak's Woodinville enterprise, roughly 20,000 square feet of display space takes in container gardens, hanging baskets, and a wide assortment of trees, shrubs, perennials, grasses, herbs, and annuals. You can also peruse a host of garden ornaments, statuary, and furniture.

Enjoy the nursery Web site's three-and-a-half-minute virtual tour to glean an overall impression of the property's layout and offerings. An illustrative map allows you to click on numbered areas to preview choice plant specimens and to see a range of products you'll find in the Home & Gift department and the Everlastings section.

Molbak's presents colorful seasonal arrays that change twice yearly, with blooming bulbs energizing the surroundings in spring and summer. Locals look forward to the Dig into Spring Celebration and the Poinsettia Festival later in the year.

Free seminars and demonstrations take place most weekends, along with activities planned especially for children, so be sure to check the Web site for a calendar of special events.

❁ **Admission:** Free.

Garden open: Sunday through Friday 10:00 A.M. to 6:00 P.M., Saturday 9:00 A.M. to 6:00 P.M.; extended hours from April through June and from mid-November through December. Call to confirm hours.

Further information: Molbak's is fully wheelchair accessible, including parking, restrooms, water fountain, etc.

Directions: Located about twenty miles northeast of Seattle. A map and driving directions are available on the Web site.

Bainbridge Island, Kitsap, and Olympic Peninsula Gardenwalks

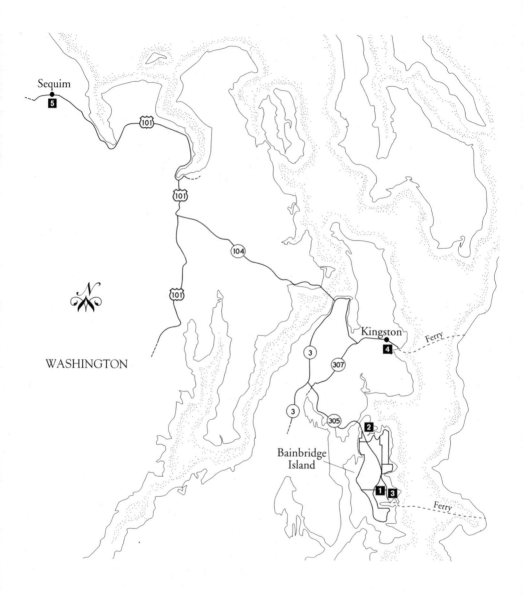

1. Bainbridge Island: Bainbridge
   Public Library Gardens
2. Bainbridge Island: The Bloedel
   Reserve
3. Bainbridge Island: Little and
   Lewis Garden Gallery

4. Kingston: Heronswood Nursery
   Ltd.
5. Sequim: Cedarbrook Herb Farm

1. Bainbridge Public Library Gardens

1270 Madison Avenue North, **Bainbridge Island,** WA 98110;
(206) 842–4162

*G*IFTED horticulturist and prolific garden writer Ann Lovejoy guides the "Friday Tidy" group of keen volunteer gardeners who tend the library's streetside gardens for all to enjoy.

The convivial participants engage in a hands-on learning experience, from soil preparation to the design aspects of combining plants. While gaining knowledge of gardening skills, they beautify the neighborhood!

In addition to exuberant perennial borders, the gardens include the haiku garden, donated by the Bainbridge Island Japanese American Community with local nursery owner Junkoh Harui, and the fern garden, donated by local landscape designer John Vandenmeerendonk with the support of the national Hardy Fern Foundation.

✿ **Admission:** Free.

Garden open: Daily around-the-clock.

Further information: There is wheelchair access to all the garden areas.

Directions: Bainbridge Island is located just west of Seattle, about one hour's travel time. Ferries leave Seattle approximately every forty minutes. Crossing time is thirty minutes. You should arrive at the Seattle ferry terminal approximately forty-five minutes to an hour before projected departure.

The library is on the southeast corner of Madison Avenue North and High School Road, 1 block east of Highway 305 in Winslow. Driving directions to the Bainbridge branch of the Kitsap Regional Library can be found on the Web at www.krl.org.

2. The Bloedel Reserve

7571 Northeast Dolphin Drive, **Bainbridge Island,** WA 98110;
(206) 842–7631; www.bloedelreserve.org

A UNIQUE, enthralling landscape, the Bloedel Reserve
should be at the top of your list when planning an itinerary
of Pacific Northwest gardens. Rather than attempt to fully recount
the property's history or to encapsulate the reserve's governing
philosophy as set forth by Prentice Bloedel, I urge you to read the
commentary in the *Self-Guided Walking Tour* pamphlet available
at the Bloedel Reserve gatehouse. Containing informative background material, the pamphlet provides a fitting orientation before
you embark on a tour of the reserve.

Presently, the Bloedel Reserve includes 150 acres, featuring
approximately 70 developed acres amid the reserve's forested
grounds. Ties to the timber industry provided the resources when
Prentice and Virginia Bloedel first purchased a home and extensive
acreage on the northern tip of Bainbridge Island in the early 1950s.
Perhaps these same associations inspired Mr. and Mrs. Bloedel, who
devoted the next thirty-five years to contemplating, planning, and
ultimately establishing the Bloedel Reserve, a complex, evolving
landscape of rare beauty. The Bloedel Reserve is currently managed
by the Arbor Fund, a nonprofit foundation set up by the Bloedels.

From the beginning, Prentice Bloedel had a profound sensitivity to the overall site, to conservation
issues, to the use of space, and to other aesthetic
concerns. He created one of the coun-
try's most lyrical landscapes and
inspired the course of development for the deeply symbiotic
environment. Today the reserve
is a place where garden travelers
might revel in the majesty of nature

while appreciating the restrained beauty of imperturbable garden scenes.

When you check in at the reserve, you'll be given a map of all the main and secondary trails. An exploration of the property will take you through settings of picturesque radiance, commencing with a meadow leading to the Bird Marsh. Here, at a point where lovely ponds and plantings culminate in an inviting wildlife habitat, you can view the commingling of natural wetlands with a planned bird refuge. A trestle footbridge farther along leads into pristine woodland. If you continue, a boardwalk shepherds you through a forest wetland.

After a relaxed stroll around the area known as the Mid Pond, you'll come upon the stately house that Mr. and Mrs. Bloedel purchased in 1952 and currently serves as the visitor center. During a July sojourn, I stood on the east side of the building looking out toward Puget Sound, savoring the sweeping vista unfolding before me. Lushly planted with Saint-John's-wort, the contour of the lofty East Bluff effected an ebullient spectacle. At one time the bluff was lowered 15 feet to enhance the stunning view. The bluff's bright carpet of sunny flowers tempered the setting's formal aspects and introduced a cheery note of surprise and wonder to the reserve's landscape.

The gardens of the Bloedel Reserve reveal a horticultural panorama of exotic and native species, with sensational varieties of trees, shrubs, perennials, and bulbs. You can admire lovely garden features, including the Moss Steps and the waterfall areas. Stroll through the Glen, distinguished by its extraordinary array of hardy cyclamen, in bloom from late August through September. Follow the Orchid Trail and soon you'll discover a small secluded spot underscored by the placement of a bench and its lovely view of the swan pond. A birthday present from Mr. Bloedel to Mrs. Bloedel, this intimate garden was designed by Geoffrey Rausch.

Bainbridge in Bloom Garden Tour

Although garden tours truly abound these days, Bainbridge in Bloom stands out as a premier model for tours nationwide.

Benefitting a fine organization (the Bainbridge Island Arts and Humanities Council), the annual Bainbridge in Bloom Garden Tour takes place in July. The seemingly boundless energy of the area's gardeners is exemplified in the five sophisticated gardens showcased. You'll recognize qualities that set apart the Pacific Northwest gardening community, like design savvy coupled with an unerring ability to create tantalizing plantings. Landscapes graced by stunning views of Puget Sound add another level of excitement for garden tourists.

Additional features are often scheduled in conjunction with the garden tour. Luncheons and lectures, book and plant sales, an art fair, and a delightful private preview party all expand on the gala atmosphere.

The island is a short ferry ride from Seattle. When you arrive on Bainbridge for the garden tour, a free tour shuttle awaits. Throughout the weekend, the shuttles arrive at the Seattle-Bainbridge ferries and make stops at designated Park & Ride locations.

For more information you can contact the council directly (221 Winslow Way West, Suite 201, Bainbridge Island, WA 98110; 206–842–7901). Or visit the Web site at www.gardentour.info, where the tour dates are posted, gardens are described, and transportation, dining, and lodging details are available. Click on Links to find ferry schedules, Kitsap public transit information, and more. Tour tickets often sell out in advance, and prices increase after May 15, so you may wish to purchase tickets from the Web site or charge tickets by phone at (206) 219–3182.

When you have completed a tour of the Orchid Trail, the harmonious juncture of the Japanese Garden, the Guest House, and the Zen Garden emerges. Remembering these gardens, I find that certain details remain vivid. One particularly elegant arrangement made me appreciate the expressive quality of unlike elements: In a flawless combination of hardscaping and flora, the Japanese Garden's stone walkway—made of smooth dark rocks set into a field of white concrete—is complemented by the contrasting, somber, and graceful blades of black lilyturf planted alongside. This design feature creates a textural cadence that soothes and stimulates the senses at the same time.

Just beyond the stone walk stands an extraordinary, luminous katsura tree with its golden autumn color. The tree's scent has been compared to hot toffee and is said to occur when the leaves fall, so that the tree emits a sweet fragrance for a considerable distance.

Utterly still, the enclosed realm known as the Reflection Pool suggests a glorious opportunity for repose. I recall pausing to rest there on a pleasant bench, contemplating the unparalleled elegance of the yew hedge, the lawn, and the rectangular pool from my vantage point. With its quiet majesty, the Reflection Pool epitomized for me the Bloedels' illustrious legacy. The reserve will deeply nourish the spirit and awaken the imagination of all garden visitors, just as it did for me.

Keep in mind, the peak period for outstanding displays of blooms at the Bloedel Reserve is April and May for trilliums, magnolias, rhododendrons, azaleas, camellias, anemones, empress trees, flowering crab apples, and cherries, among others. In May and June you'll enjoy primroses, lungworts, flowering dogwoods, and Solomon's seal. In September and October look for *Kirengeshoma*, adorned with lovely nodding clusters of waxy yellow flowers.

✿ **Admission:** Fee.

    Garden open: Wednesday through Sunday 10:00 A.M. to 4:00 P.M.; closed federal holidays. Call to schedule a visit; reservations are required.

    Further information: Visit the Web site to see a map and to learn more about special events taking place at the Bloedel Reserve. Tour guides are available for groups by prior arrangement. Wheelchairs are available by reservation. Much of the garden is wheelchair accessible; some portions are not due to steps or steepness of trails.

Directions: The reserve is on the north end of Bainbridge Island, a fifteen-minute drive from the ferry terminal to Seattle. You can download directions from the Web site.

3. Little and Lewis Garden Gallery

1940 Wing Point Way NE, **Bainbridge Island,** WA 98110;
(206) 842–8327; www.littleandlewis.com

*T*HEATRICALITY, artistry, and an extravagant jungle of plants come together in the garden and gallery of Little and Lewis, creating a tantalizing atmosphere of superabundance.

When George Little and David Lewis joined forces some fifteen years ago, they set about designing and installing ponds. Since that time Little and Lewis have grown to be plantsmen nonpareil, while their creative partnership has led to an exceptional body of sculptural works.

As you enter the garden's main gate, you'll find fountains, pools, and inventive water features emerging at every turn, along with potent sculptures that contribute to the expressive character of this fanciful realm.

The muted blues, rusty terra-cotta, and pale copper greens of the concrete sculptures created by Little and Lewis—audacious gunnera leaves, Tuscan columns with textured surfaces, the whimsical form of the "Raintree" upholstered in baby's tears—play off lavish alliances of semitropical and hardy plant specimens.

In a garden pulsing with the murmurs and splashes of falling water and lively jets, you'll be overcome by the bold plantings. The paddlelike leaves of statuesque bananas and beguiling textures of architectural tree ferns provide structure in the garden. George and David overwinter many of the most tender specimens in their greenhouse, so once the growing season begins anew each year, the plants reemerge in their full glory.

The garden/gallery surroundings overflow with enchanting plant marriages. For instance, the soft blue-green hue of an agave yields to a golden catalpa (*Catalpa bignonioides* 'Aurea') displaying huge butter-yellow leaves. The tree is given a hard pruning each season to achieve the dramatic foliage.

A trove of flowering specimens flourish; scarlet *Crocosmia* 'Lucifer' and the whorled citron blooms of *Lysimachia punctata* 'Alexander' introduce beaming hues amid an aspect of antiquity conveyed by the color-washed columns supporting a pergola.

It's interesting to note that David once worked on archaeological digs in Greece, and George holds a fascination with Minoan and Meso-American architecture. Such influences intermingle with botanical themes, then materialize as concepts behind many of the artworks.

As you meander through the garden, you'll discover an intriguing portal framing a more subdued, sheltered area. Here the cardinal-red blooms of a hybrid epiphyllum light up verdant green surroundings.

Beyond, in a shady corner, the carefully placed Raintree water feature appears, weeping continuous droplets that stir the surface of a little pool beneath.

The visually rich milieu created by these artist-gardener collaborators represents a gem among the Pacific Northwest's many nuanced garden environments. Meriting a special place on the national horticultural landscape, it sparkles with equal brilliance on the international scene.

A multifaceted experience awaits when you enter this unique oasis on Bainbridge Island's Wing Point Way. In the meantime, you can enjoy previewing the evocative sculpture and arresting gardening style that has had such an impact on garden makers from near and far. A new book published by Timber Press, *A Garden Gallery: The Plants, Art, and Hardscape of Little and Lewis*, is filled with alluring photographs and with a stimulating narrative by David and George.

❁ **Admission:** Free for individuals; there is a charge for garden clubs and groups determined by the number of people in the party.

Garden open: Seasonally by appointment only. Call or visit the Web site for dates and times. Several times a year the garden/gallery can be visited on special open days. It also opens in conjunction with the Bainbridge Island Garden Tour; see the sidebar in this chapter for details about this popular tour. Clients interested in purchasing sculpture may schedule an appointment year-round.

Further information: The Web site contains dates and details to help arrange your visit. A few curbs and narrow paths result in partial wheelchair accessibility.

Directions: The garden is thirty minutes from Seattle via an auto ferry ride. You can also approach by land from the South Sound, using Highways 3 and 305. Driving directions are found on the Web site.

4. Heronswood Nursery Ltd.

7530 Northeast 288th Street, **Kingston,** WA 98346;
(360) 297-4172; www.heronswood.com

*I*NAUGURATED in 1990, Heronswood has achieved national prominence to a degree that owners of other plant nurseries can only imagine in their dreams. The nursery successfully combines the considerable talents of founding partners Dan Hinkley and Robert Jones. A former horticulture professor, Hinkley uses his expert's touch in the skillful collecting, propagating, and proliferating of unusually regal specimens desired by connoisseurs. Jones, trained as an architect, now applies his acumen to the management of the business details.

Appease your lust for rare plants by planning a journey to Heronswood, located in the arcadian wonderland of Kingston,

Washington. The region's remarkable climate allows plants to develop with otherworldly vigor. Avid gardeners from near and far come here to explore the multitude of rare shrubs and exemplary perennials, the spectacular trees for their fall color and fine form, and the splendid ornamental vines.

At Heronswood's highly touted province of flora, you will find offerings that are unequaled elsewhere. The plant selections include recently discovered rarities resulting from Dan's plant expeditions to places such as Nepal, the Sea of Japan, China and North Vietnam. Tour the lush display gardens and you will see mature plantings that demonstrate endless ideas for beautiful plant combinations.

The woodland gardens are perfection. Look for lovely compositions, like the luminous foliage and graceful, outstretched branches of a golden locust hovering over a medley of shrubs and herbaceous perennials. Strolling the paths, I was transfixed by the strangely beautiful jack-in-the-pulpits (*Arisaema*), with their startling inflorescences. These popular plants are a fine example of the abundance associated with Heronswood; there were twenty-four different selections to choose from in an earlier catalog. At the time this entry was written, forty-five species were available from the nursery! Among the exciting choices is one species boasting marbled pewter foliage and another that stands out for its purple-and-white striped spathes.

In the Potager, look for the strapping *Rheum palmatum*, an ornamental rhubarb! The billowy perennial borders and luxuriant containers display a range of exciting plants, including ones dubbed "temperennials." While some of these plants are hardy enough to survive cold winters, others are too tender to winter over. These specimens introduce notes of texture and color to the summer garden—from furry, silvery lime leaves, to plummy-purple foliage and bright golden bronze flowers.

A showcase for skillfully executed garden design, Heronswood's gardens flawlessly integrate lyrical plantings with stunning hardscaping, sparkling water features, and discrete ornamentation. Adorning the gardens are metal sculptures by Mark Bulwinkle and the magnificent "ruin"—pillars capped with terra-cotta planters and a "chanterelle" fountain executed by Little and Lewis of Bainbridge Island (see the previous gardenwalk).

In an area replete with great gardens blessed by a climate affording ample moisture and moderate temperatures, the artistry of Heronswood's gardens promises to inspire the designer in each of us to bolder, more inventive plantings.

Gardeners . . . be sure to get a copy of Heronswood's richly descriptive, gloriously colorful free catalog. To do so, e-mail info@ heronswood.com, or you may call, fax, or write to have your name added to the mailing list.

✤ **Admission:** Fee.

Garden open: By appointment or on Garden Open Days, as noted in the Heronswood catalog and on the Web site. Closed holidays.

Further information: The nursery is open by appointment most Tuesdays through Fridays and many Saturdays. Call ahead to schedule a visit. While there, visitors are welcome to shop and walk the gardens. Guided tours are provided for $100 per hour for small groups of up to twenty people. Heronswood also offers an excellent schedule of seminars that run throughout spring, summer, and autumn along with Saturday "walk and shop" tours, workshops, and classes for young people. Check the Web site for the latest schedule or call (360) 297–4172 or fax (360) 297–8321. Wheelchair accessibility is limited.

Directions: Heronswood is located on the north end of the Kitsap Peninsula, northwest of Seattle. Kingston is about twenty-five minutes from the Bainbridge Ferry Terminal, ten minutes from the Kingston Ferry Terminal, one and a half hours from Seattle (including ferry time), and four hours from Portland. Detailed directions to the nursery can be found on the Web site.

5. Cedarbrook Herb Farm

1345 South Sequim Avenue, **Sequim,** WA 98382; (800) 470–8423, (360) 783–7733; www.cedarbrookherbfarm.com

*C*EDARBROOK HERB FARM is touted as the state of Washington's first herb farm, and the establishment's many admirers can attest to the glories of the alluring lavender fields that are currently one of the highlights of the twelve-acre farm. Some seventy varieties of lavender, an impressive collection to be sure, are available for purchase.

Exuberant arrays of flowers, mainly drought-tolerant specimens, surround the property's charming one-hundred-year-old farmhouse. Originally known as Bell House, the historical building was the homestead of James Bell, the son of Sequim's earliest settler. Other legacies of the Bell family are the plantings that remain nearby the house to this day, including old lilacs, flowering quince bushes, and Gravenstein apple trees.

Proprietor Toni Anderson has been inspired by the impressionist painter Claude Monet. His influence is seen in the vibrant planting style of the farm's colorful display gardens. The drought-tolerant plants make sense when you learn that Sequim is situated in the rain shadow of the Olympic Mountains. Toni explains; "It's called the Blue Hole. It can be pouring rain in Seattle, but there will be no rain in Sequim. You can see a line about a mile outside of town where it will be lighter, even if the sun isn't shining."

Browse through the gift shop, housed in the farmhouse, and take in the heady scent of lavender sachets, wreaths, wands, and essential oils, along with a range of culinary products and other gifts.

Then follow the garden's meandering gravel pathways. You'll discover a beguiling, rustic arbor apparently crafted of driftwood. The

Sequim Lavender Festival

The Sequim Lavender Growers Association hosts a delightful celebration of everything lavender on the third weekend of each July on Washington's North Olympic Peninsula.

The city of Sequim (pronounced S'kwim) boasts the title of the Lavender Capital of North America. And rightly so, as the growers association encompasses an ever-increasing organization of farmers who specialize in growing the fragrant herb.

Farm tours are a highlight of the festival. They provide opportunities to explore a select number of lavender farms and chat with the growers. Certainly you'll wish to wallow in the farms' beguiling gardens, with their atmospheric haze of blooming lavender varieties, and stroll among fields rich with the herb's heady scent. Gift shops at each of the farms featured on the tour offer excellent selections of handcrafted gifts and culinary products made with the ancient, aromatic plant.

A street fair held in downtown Sequim is another of the festival's programs, and one enjoyed by visitors and the surrounding community alike. The street celebration is located on Fir Street, between Sequim and Third Avenues.

Festival support buttons can be purchased at the street fair's information booths, the Sequim visitor information kiosk, and at the farms included on the tour; children under age twelve are admitted free. The button is your admission to all the farms on tour for the three days of the festival. The button also provides free rides on the farm tour buses. Each farm has limited parking, should you choose to drive to the tour farms. No admission is charged for the street fair, which features food, music, a wine and beer garden, and more than one hundred vendor booths.

Look on the festival Web site (www.lavenderfestival.com) for printable maps, directions, and links that provide details for air travel, motorcoach, ferries, and car rentals. Or call (877) 681–3035 for toll-free festival information. To learn about lavender events scheduled year-round, visit www.lavendergrowers.org.

eye-catching garden ornament was actually constructed by a local artisan who employed wonderfully gnarly sections of old cedar root.

Continue exploring and you'll come upon another more traditional painted arbor beckoning you to breathe in the fragrant atmosphere of myriad herbs.

❀ **Admission:** Free.

Garden open: Daily; call for seasonal summer and winter hours. Closed December 24 through January 15.

Further information: Petal's Garden Café serves lunch and dinner Sunday through Thursday 11:00 A.M. to 8:00 P.M., Friday and Saturday 11:00 A.M. to 9:00 P.M. Cedarbrook Herb Farm participates in the annual Sequim Lavender Festival. Wheelchair accessibility is limited.

Directions: Take U.S. Highway 101 to Sequim. Sequim Avenue runs right through the town. Take the Sequim Avenue exit south toward the mountains, and you'll find Cedarbrook Herb Farm ¼ mile up the hill on the right.

South Puget Sound Gardenwalks

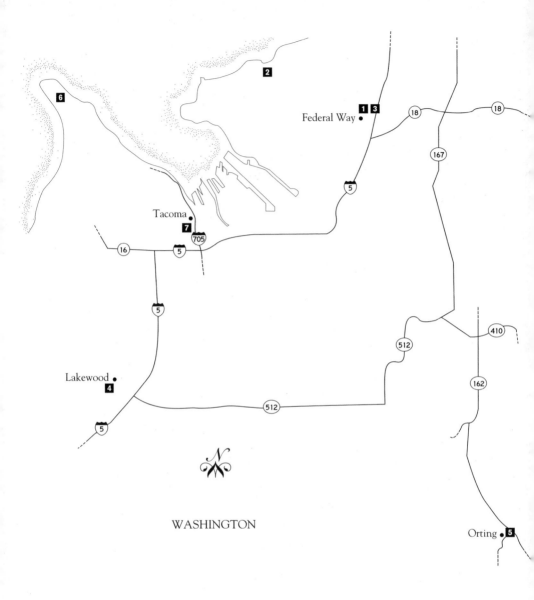

2

6

Federal Way ● **1** **3**

Tacoma ●
7

Lakewood ●
4

WASHINGTON

Orting ● **5**

1. Pacific Rim Bonsai Collection

Weyerhaeuser Company, 33663 Weyerhaeuser Way South,
Federal Way, WA 98003; (253) 924–5206;
www.weyerhaeuser.com/bonsai

A FASCINATING collection of masterful bonsai specimens is yours to behold at the Weyerhaeuser Company's corporate headquarters campus in Federal Way. The headquarters building is a magnificent example of corporate architecture, and the Weyerhaeuser grounds are notable for the breathtaking landscape design by landscape architects Sasaki, Walker and Associates and project leader Peter Walker.

Opened in 1989 as a permanent exhibition, the Pacific Rim Bonsai Collection is appropriately described in the Weyerhaeuser Company's literature as an outdoor museum of living art. The collection is surrounded by a pristine wooded area highlighted by Douglas firs. The one-acre display site itself benefits from the handsome design work of Thomas L. Berger of Thomas L. Berger Associates.

Exhibited in a tropical conservatory and on outdoor tables, the Pacific Rim Bonsai Collection is given a partial sense of enclosure by stucco walls that function as elegant backdrops for groupings of two or three bonsai. Among the exceptional bonsai shown are plants from China, Japan, Korea, Taiwan, the United States, and Canada. Visitors come from across the U.S. and abroad to admire these remarkable specimens.

Don't miss this collection when planning a travel itinerary of gardens in the Seattle area. A free guidebook gives information about the history of bonsai and the philosophical and artistic concepts on which it is based. A section entitled "Questions and

A Closer Look at Bonsai

A millenniums-old art form, bonsai traces its roots to ancient China, when creating and cultivating a garden was a praiseworthy pursuit and where the production of glazed ceramics made available beautiful vessels in which to plant exotic specimens. The word *bonsai* first emerged around A.D. 400 in a Chinese poem, while a mural from a tomb that dates back 1200 years ago depicts the image of a gift of a bonsai. In centuries past representations of various types of bonsai appear in Japan to illustrate rare manuscripts.

Landscape and tree bonsai are the two general classifications studied. In the landscape form, rocks often dominate, in combination with trees and such decorative touches as bridges, boats, and figures.

Shape, height, and species are taken into consideration when classifying tree bonsai, along with elements such as broadleaf or coniferous evergreens and flowering or fruiting trees. The number of trees makes up another category, from single-trunk specimens to arrangements with multiple trunks or a group of trees.

To cultivate bonsai, one must appreciate the importance of repotting specimens, for healthy plants require root pruning and refreshed soil in the proper proportions.

Taking on the role of artist, the bonsai gardener strives above all for harmony, looking to the unity between a tree and its pot to achieve the sought-after aesthetic effect.

Answers about Bonsai" explains some of the horticultural principles and technical processes utilized in bonsai design. The guidebook will help visitors appreciate the high level of artistry and technical skill represented in the trees on display.

The Pacific Rim Bonsai Collection presents a unique opportunity to explore a wealth of plants imbued with the profound cultural associations of Asian art and society. Quietly experience these bonsai, and you'll become in tune with their rare beauty and symbolic grace.

One bonsai of special note that you will generally find on display is number 102. It represents the best characteristics of two different species. This masterpiece was achieved by grafting or fusing the branch tips and foliage of a Chinese juniper to the trunk and branches of an ancient living Sierra juniper. Estimated to be between 800 and 1,000 years old, it is the collection's oldest tree.

The Domoto trident maple (number 109), another historically significant bonsai in the collection, has been cultivated as a bonsai for about 125 years. At 6½ feet tall, the tree's unusually large stature tells a fascinating story. Toichi Domoto inherited the bonsai from his father, who purchased it at the close of the 1915 Panama-Pacific International Exposition in San Francisco, where it had been on display. Forced to leave his home during World War II, Domoto was interned briefly, but because of his high level of education, he found employment in the Chicago area. Domoto continued to pay his Washington real estate taxes, and he was able to pay someone to water the bonsai. Thus, during the four years that Toichi Domoto was not allowed to return to his Federal Way home, the tree grew unchecked and the roots of the bonsai grew down through the drainage holes of its container into the earth. Today the tree grows in a custom-made Chinese container that is, by volume, the largest bonsai container in the United States.

❀ **Admission:** Free.

    Garden open: Friday through Wednesday 10:00 A.M. to 4:00 P.M. from March through September; Saturday through Wednesday 11:00 A.M. to 4:00 P.M. from October through February. Call to confirm seasonal hours.

    Further information: Individual garden visitors are welcome. Free guided tours are offered to the public each Sunday at noon; no reservations are required. Call (253) 924-3153 to make an appointment for a free guided tour for groups of ten or more. Visit the Web site to see a current schedule of programs featuring bonsai lectures, special events, and exhibits. There is full wheelchair accessibility.

Directions: Federal Way is about thirty minutes south of Seattle, off Interstate 5, just northeast of Tacoma. Signs direct you to the Pacific Rim Bonsai Collection. Complete driving directions and a map are found on the Web site.

2. PowellsWood—A Northwest Garden

430 South Dash Point Road, **Federal Way,** WA (mailing address: 29607 Eighth Avenue South, Federal Way, WA 98003); (253) 529-1620; www.powellswood.org

*M*ONTE AND DIANE Powell have created a remarkable private garden on the site of a previously vacant and weedy lot in the Marine Hills section of Federal Way, bordering Puget Sound.

The PowellsWood garden occupies its own three-acre corner within a greater forty-acre property that encompasses the Powells' home. Two years were spent eradicating brush and preparing the soil for planting before the lovely garden of today could even begin to take shape.

Landscape architect Ned Gulbran assisted the Powells in the design process, structuring the layout of garden rooms. The Powells called upon Sue Buckles to help produce the atmospheric effects of the perennial borders.

PowellsWood's overall scheme boasts a winding stream and pond that incorporate storm water channeled to drain into Puget Sound. Some 1,000 types of trees, blossoming shrubs, and plants of all sorts beautify the cultivated landscape. A woodland garden was completed in 2002, followed by the patio area. The Garden Room serves as a place for classes and a gathering spot for community gardening groups.

Visitors also discover that much of the Powells' land remains in its native, forested state, while the surrounding locale yields to densely populated urban development. Demonstrating a very different scenario, PowellsWood is a once-envisioned garden sanctuary come into being. And garden travelers are invited to visit.

✿ **Admission:** Fee.

Garden open: By appointment; call or e-mail admin@powellswood.org. The garden is open to the public on Mother's Day weekend and on Wednesday and Thursday 10:00 A.M. to 2:00 P.M. from April 1 through October 15. Additionally, the garden opens in conjunction with the Garden Conservancy Open Days Program; see the resources chapter for details.

Further information: Most areas of the garden are accessible via lawns and cobbled or graveled walkways. Sturdy walking shoes are advised for all who plan to explore the garden fully.

Directions: PowellsWood is about thirty minutes south of Seattle if you avoid rush traffic. Detailed driving directions and a map are on the Web site.

3. Rhododendron Species Foundation and Botanical Garden

2525 South 336th Street, **Federal Way,** WA 98003 (mailing address: P.O. Box 3798, Federal Way, WA 98063); (253) 661-9377; www.rhodygarden.org

*O*PERATED BY the Rhododendron Species Foundation, this botanical garden features twenty-two acres devoted to the display and conservation of more than 435 species of *Rhododendron*.

Several hundred types of companion plants embellish the 10,000 plants growing in a woodland setting. To enjoy the peak bloom time, visit the garden mid-March through mid-May for a brilliant exhibition. In summer expect to find late-blooming rhododendrons, lilies, hydrangeas, and ferns. Carnivorous plants are an added delight.

The garden's fall colors call attention to azaleas, maples, fothergillas, and a wide array of other trees and shrubs.

Wintry profiles of deciduous trees and the handsome forms and foliage of conifers are a laudable sight, while early-blooming types of rhododendron and textural heathers enliven the surroundings from early January through February.

❀ **Admission:** Fee from March through October; free from November through February.

Garden open: Friday through Wednesday 10:00 A.M. to 4:00 P.M. from March through May; Saturday through Wednesday 11:00 A.M. to 4:00 P.M. from June through February. Gift shop is open Saturday through Wednesday 11:00 A.M. to 4:00 P.M. Call to confirm hours.

Further information: Check the Web site for a calendar of events or to learn about plant sales. Call to arrange a guided tour, which requires a minimum of fifteen participants. Restrooms and the gift shop are fully wheelchair accessible.

Directions: The foundation and garden are on the Weyerhaeuser Corporate Headquarters Campus, adjacent to the Pacific Rim Bonsai Collection (see the earlier entry). Take I–5 south from Seattle to exit 143; turn left (east) onto South 320th Street. Turn onto Weyerhaeuser Way South and continue through the roundabout. Follow Weyerhaeuser Company signs to the bonsai garden parking area. Call for additional detailed directions or look on the Web site.

4. Lakewold Gardens

12317 Gravelly Lake Drive SW, **Lakewood,** WA 98499;
(888) 858–4106; www.lakewold.org

A GRAND ESTATE garden that was once home to Eulalie and Corydon Wagner, the historic Lakewold Gardens encompass some ten acres and feature the design work of the celebrated landscape architect Thomas Church.

Eulalie Wagner's vision combined beautifully with Church's refined aesthetic, resulting in a delightful melding of naturalistic areas with an exquisite layout of formal garden rooms. Mrs. Wagner's gift of the gardens to the nonprofit Friends of Lakewold ensured that this lovely landscape and house would be preserved for the public's enjoyment as well as for educational purposes.

Remodeled in the 1950s, the Wagners' former home reflects the Georgian style. Distinguished by its wisteria-draped veranda, the mansion enjoys fine views of Gravelly Lake and Mount Rainier.

The gardens' original circular driveway is thought to have been designed by the Olmsted Brothers of Massachusetts. Azaleas and bevies of rhododendron bloom here and along the walk to the house.

As you explore the gardens, you will come upon parterres, topiary ornamentation, and an Elizabethan knot garden. The brick walkway, laid out in a fine herringbone pattern, goes from the mansion to a high point of the formal gardens—a belvedere adorned with climbing roses. Another stunning feature emerges off to the side, where a quatrefoil pool manifests the classic markings of a Church design.

The woodland area enlivened by waterfalls and a scree garden highlighting gray alpine plants are noteworthy features.

Lakewold Gardens' exceptional collection of Japanese maples beautifies the property, working in consort with mature specimens such as empress tree, dawn redwood, yellow flowering cherries, copper beech, bristlecone pine, and the dove tree (*Davidia involucrata*), with its glowing white bracts that look like handkerchiefs.

❀ **Admission:** Fee.

Garden open: Wednesday through Sunday 10:00 A.M. to 4:00 P.M. from April through September; Friday through Sunday 10:00 A.M. to 3:00 P.M. from October through March. Call to confirm hours. The garden shop is open during regular hours.

Further information: Visitors can enjoy self-guided tours of Lakewold; check the Web site for detailed lists of what's in bloom at various times. Call in advance to reserve a docent-led tour for ten or more individuals. The garden shop carries books and tools along with plants and gift items. Wheelchair access is limited.

Directions: Lakewold is 40 miles south of Seattle and 10 miles south of the Tacoma Dome. From I–5, take exit 124. Turn west onto Gravelly Lake Drive SW and proceed approximately 1 mile. Look for the entrance to Lakewold on your right after the stoplight at Veterans Drive SW. Detailed driving directions and a map are on the Web site.

5. The Chase Garden

16015 264th Street East, **Orting**, WA 98360; (206) 242–4040; www.chasegarden.org

*S*ITUATED ON a bluff and enhanced by sublime views of the Puyallup River Valley and Mount Rainier, the four-and-a-half-acre Chase Garden has been lovingly attended to by Emmott and Ione Chase for more than four decades.

At the start the Chases embarked on clearing the land of brush and tree stumps, taking great care to protect the property's magnificent second-growth conifers. They towed rocks, turned the soil, propagated plants, and toiled hard to create a lovely gardenscape.

The results of their efforts shine forth in a harmonious landscape articulated in classic Pacific Northwest garden style.

An organic pattern of meandering paths emerged when Ione Chase began sculpting the terrain. She called upon landscape architect A. Rex Zumwalt to assist in designing the area closest to the house. Zumwalt's touch influenced the entrance garden, endowing it with stylistic elements of a Japanese garden: free-flowing planting beds, reflecting pools, a dry stream, and artful raked gravel.

Admirers often comment upon the Chase Garden's seamless melding of a Japanese design sensibility with a regional aesthetic that has evolved over time and prospered. While it demonstrates modernist tendencies, this aesthetic embraces a naturalistic approach. The guiding principle expresses reverence for the setting's native flora and the extraordinary scenery.

Appearing linked to the surrounding vegetation, the garden takes in woodland plantings, a rock garden, and an alpine meadow. In springtime, the garden's vitality is obvious.

A glorious evergreen canopy of firs, western red cedars, and hemlocks presides over the wooded area, where thriving native species include vanilla leaf, *Trillium ovatum*, *Erythronium*, and false Solomon's seal. These give rise to gemlike blooms that brighten the fertile environment.

Look to the gentle, curving configuration of the meadow as one of the garden's most graceful landscape vignettes. Ione Chase masterfully combined a patchwork of specimens that glow with blooms from mid-April into June. Heaths and heathers commingle with geraniums, gentians, and dianthus, delineating colorful swatches for an effective vista.

Another special spot to seek out is the Lewisia Allée. Chase cultivates *Lewisia cotyledon* in a location under the eaves of her house. The plants are shielded from winter rains and thus can flourish without the snow cover that coddles the species in its mountainous habitat. Commonly known as Siskiyou bitterroot, the plants produce fleshy rosettes of leaves set off by showy flowers, white to pink and generally striped, carried on upright stems.

As a project of the Garden Conservancy, the lyrical Chase Garden is worthy of your support. Members enjoy particular benefits, such as an invitation to visit early in the year, when visitors take delight in displays of snowdrops and other early bloomers.

❊ **Admission:** Fee.

Garden open: By appointment only on select days from mid-April to mid-June. Also open in conjunction with the Garden Conservancy's Open Days Program; see the resources chapter.

Further information: The Web site provides up-to-date news, a calendar of events, membership information, and tour details. Call or e-mail to reserve your docent-led tours for individuals or groups. You may also click on the Reservation Requests link on the Web site. Wheelchair access is limited.

Directions: The Chase Garden is an hour south of Seattle in Pierce County. Directions are given when you make your reservation.

6. Point Defiance Park Gardens

5400 North Pearl Street, **Tacoma**, WA; (253) 305–1010; www.metroparkstacoma.org

*T*HE VAST parkland of Point Defiance Park embraces areas of natural forest with hiking paths, saltwater beaches, and alluring views across Puget Sound.

Delightful cultivated spaces also await your visit. Enter the park off Pearl Street at Park Avenue and the eye-catching architecture of a pagoda emerges. Modeled after a seventeenth-century Japanese structure, the pagoda serves as the centerpiece of the park's Japanese Garden, where springtime displays of flowering cherries, crab apples, azaleas, and rhododendrons vivify the area. Artfully placed pine trees, water features, and a charming footbridge ornament the tranquil scenery year-round.

The Rose Garden, situated nearby, is not to be missed. The garden dates from 1895, when many types of roses were planted. Its present-day oval layout took shape in 1913, and today the refurbished setting takes in more than an acre of grassy expanses highlighted by an appealing, centrally placed gazebo adorned with climbing roses. Hybrid teas, floribundas, and grandifloras commingle with old garden roses.

Bordering the main area, a newer garden of miniature roses encircles a wishing well. The bloom in the Rose Garden begins in May, while the miniature varieties are most entrancing in June and July. Accredited as an All-America Rose Selections Display Garden, the garden's overall exhibition peaks during visits in June through September.

A host of theme gardens provide seasonal interest at Point Defiance. You'll enjoy bevies of dahlias, fuchsias, and rhododendrons. An herb garden is at its best in spring and summer. Plan also to experience the one-and-a-half-acre Northwest Native Garden, with its winding pathways that give way to a waterfall and pond. The design and placement of the garden's lovely wooden gazebo demonstrate the skillful touch of famed landscape architect Thomas Church.

❀ **Admission:** Free.

Garden open: Daily sunrise to sunset.

Further information: The Japanese Garden and Rose Garden are partially wheelchair accessible. The Dahlia Garden has wide gravel pathways. The Iris, Herb, and Fuchsia Gardens have accessible asphalt paths. The Rhododendron and Northwest Native Gardens feature hilly terrain and are not wheelchair accessible. To view a detailed map of Point Defiance Park, search www.discoverparks.org.

Directions: Located north of downtown Tacoma, Point Defiance is surrounded by Puget Sound and the Narrows.

7. W. W. Seymour Botanical Conservatory at Wright Park

316 South G Street, **Tacoma**, WA 98405; (253) 591–5330; www.metroparkstacoma.org

*W*HEN W. W. SEYMOUR founded the conservatory in Wright Park in 1908, his plan was to forge a link between the public and the wonders of the natural world. Now listed on the Tacoma, Washington State, and national historic registers, the Victorian-style conservatory is distinguished by a stunning twelve-sided central glass dome.

Lush floral displays and a collection of exotic plants promise to enliven your visit to the Tacoma area any time of the year.

The conservatory beckons with displays of showy mums and asters during the fall season. On a damp November day, take in the tropical room, where displays of hybrid chrysanthemums boast gigantic blooms and vivid colors.

December highlights include flowering narcissus that broadcast a beguiling fragrance, while the indoor atmosphere is aglow with bold amaryllis blooms. Throughout the winter months you'll find inviting arrangements of azaleas and cyclamen, orchids and clivias.

Tulips are harbingers that light up the springtime scene, along with Asiatic and Easter lilies. The show continues with hydrangeas and changing arrays of blooms spanning the summer months.

❀ **Admission:** Free; donations are appreciated.

Garden open: Tuesday through Sunday 10:00 A.M. to 4:30 P.M.; closed Thanksgiving, November 30 through December 3, December 25, and New Year's Day. The gift shop closes at 4:00 P.M.

Further information: The gift shop offers exotic plants and botanical gift items. Guided group tours are available for a fee when reserved in advance; call for details. The recently remodeled conservatory is wheelchair accessible.

Directions: Located in Tacoma's Wright Park at Sixth Avenue at South Yakima Avenue, the conservatory is situated along the park's eastern boundary. From I–5 take exit 133 (Interstate 705 north/City Center). Look for I–705 north/Schuster Parkway signs, then get in the right lane and take the Stadium Way exit. At the stoplight, turn right onto Stadium Way, and then turn left onto Fourth Street. Take Fourth Street to G Street, and turn right. You'll find a map at www .discoverparks.org.

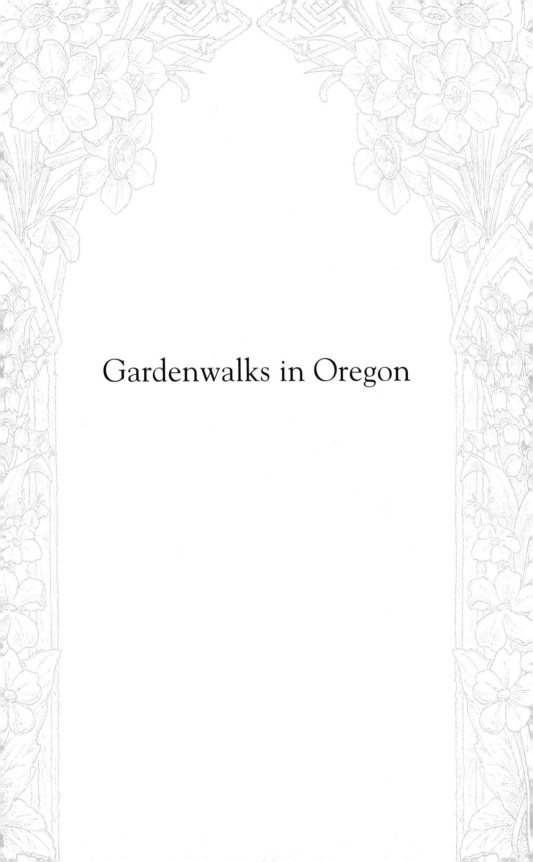

Gardenwalks in Oregon

Portland and Vicinity
Gardenwalks

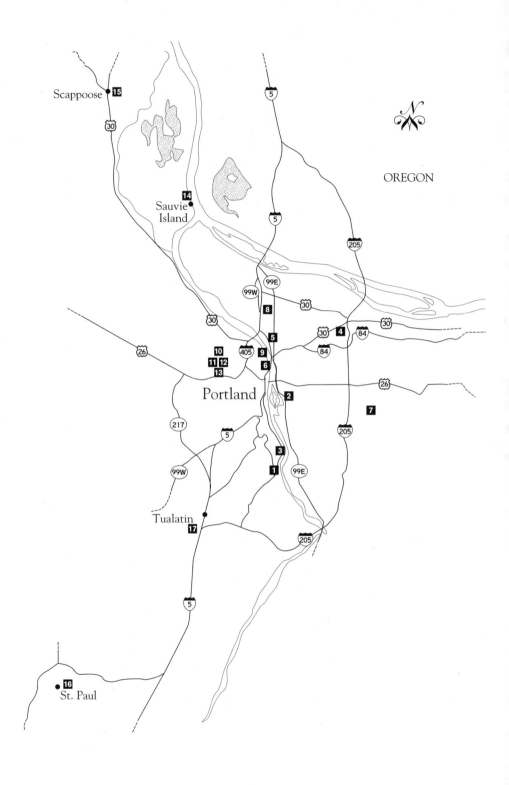

1. Portland: The Berry Botanic Garden
2. Portland: Crystal Springs Rhododendron Garden
3. Portland: Elk Rock, the Garden at the Bishop's Close
4. Portland: The Grotto
5. Portland: Hogan and Sanderson Garden
6. Portland: Ira C. Keller Memorial Fountain Park
7. Portland: Leach Botanical Garden
8. Portland: Peninsula Park Rose Garden
9. Portland: Portland Classical Chinese Garden
10. Portland: Washington Park
11. Portland: Washington Park's Hoyt Arboretum
12. Portland: Washington Park's International Rose Test Garden
13. Portland: Washington Park's Japanese Garden
14. Sauvie Island: Cistus Nursery
15. Scappoose: Joy Creek Nursery
16. St. Paul: Heirloom Roses
17. Tualatin: Kaiser Permanente's Tualatin Poison Prevention Garden

1. The Berry Botanic Garden

11505 Southwest Summerville Avenue, **Portland,** OR 97219;
(503) 636–4112; www.berrybot.org

*P*ASSIONATE gardener, exceptional plantswoman, and an inspirational figure in the world of horticulture, Rae Selling Berry prevailed over a condition of hereditary deafness and left a remarkable legacy for plant lovers. In the Berry Botanic Garden, the admirable depth and breadth of the plant collections—and the projects the garden carries out today—attest to Rae Berry's enduring spirit.

In 1938 Rae and Alfred Berry acquired the parcel of land that was destined to become the Berry Botanic Garden. The Berrys purchased this nine-acre property near the Willamette River to give Rae sufficient space to pursue propagating and cultivating the myriad specimens she wished to grow.

Seattle landscape architect John Grant assisted with siting trees and laying out the lawn, but Rae Berry took responsibility for planning and planting the areas devoted to exceptional collections of primulas and alpine plants. She also planted rhododendron species from seeds. Two particularly large types, *Rhododendron decorum* and *R. calophytum*, have matured now into what looks like a natural forest.

The Berry Botanic Garden's quarter-acre Rock Garden is most interesting. Represented here are 300 species of alpine plants from around the world, ranging from true alpines to plants that thrive in an alpine bog environment.

Stroll on the Native Plant Trail and be sure to explore the Demonstration and Water Gardens. Awaiting your discovery are nearly 200 Pacific Northwest native plants that make up one of the garden's five major collections. Look for plant labels and interpretive signs to point out examples of lady fern, red currant, Oregon grape, skunk cabbage, pitcher plant, and the lacy leaves of western bleeding heart.

In June visitors are left breathless by glorious displays of the mythic Himalayan blue poppy and the Nepalese poppy found growing in the primula beds. I was bewitched by the tall—to 5 feet—stands of dusty pink *Meconopsis napaulensis*. Your attention will also be drawn to simply stunning arrays of the alluringly soft, subtle blue-hued poppies, 'Crewsdon's hybrids'.

The genus *Primula* was one of Rae Berry's cherished favorites, and visitors will revel in the Berry Botanic Garden's profusion of primula species. Aficionados of primroses will be transported by the delightfully colorful, flowering candelabras of *Primula aurantiaca*. Another noteworthy primula, *P. cusickiana*, bears violet-scented flowers and is native to northeastern Oregon. Dubbed "Cooky" by Rae Berry, *P. cusickiana* happens to be particularly temperamental to cultivate and is known to have eluded Berry's skillful attempts to grow it. Today this plant's delightful image is used as the garden's logo. It symbolizes the Berry Botanic Garden's commitment to promoting a vast kingdom of plants.

Continuing in the tradition set forth by Rae Berry, who carefully planned various microhabitats to preserve rare plants, the Berry Botanic Garden is widely acknowledged for its praiseworthy conservation of endangered plants. The garden maintains the Seed Bank for Rare and Endangered Plants of the Pacific Northwest; engages in research; and participates in studies of imperiled species like the lovely, elegant trout lily, *Erythronium elegans*.

When you visit, pick up the handout entitled *Plants-of-Note* and follow the numbered map for your own in-depth tour of the Berry Botanic Garden's exhilarating presentation of unusual plants.

✤ **Admission:** Fee.

Garden open: Daily during daylight hours, by appointment only.

Further information: Call to schedule an appointment during office hours (Monday through Friday 9:00 A.M. to 4:30 P.M.) or call extension 43 anytime to leave a message for visitor services. You'll find a list of special events and a virtual tour available on the Web site. The garden offers partial wheelchair access.

Directions: Berry Botanic Garden is located in the hills of southwest Portland. Visit the Web site to see detailed driving directions or for public transportation information. Driving directions are also available on the garden's voice-mail system.

2. Crystal Springs Rhododendron Garden

Southeast Twenty-eighth Avenue and Woodstock Boulevard,
Portland, OR 97202; (503) 771–8386; www.portlandparks.org

*R*HODODENDRONS have thrived in Portland's temperate climate since England's Waterer Nursery first introduced the plants to the Pacific Northwest in 1905. Crystal Springs Rhododendron Garden presents an inviting landscape, cared for by a group of enthusiastic volunteers affiliated with the Rhododendron Society and assisted by the Portland Parks and Recreation Department.

Encompassing approximately five acres, Crystal Springs Rhododendron Garden is dedicated to the cultivation of these praiseworthy plants. The garden celebrates the many attributes of rhododendrons, from their fine structure and attractive leaves to their resplendent flowers. Boasting nearly 800 species and hybrid varieties, the 2,500 rhododendrons and azaleas that make up the collection at Crystal Springs include admirable specimens that are nearly one hundred years old.

The glorious display of rhododendron blooms peaks in April and May and continues into June. On Mother's Day weekend you can expect to enjoy a superior display. Among the more exotic *Rhododendron* species, *R. bureavii* exhibits an enchanting dark woolly covering on the underside of its leaves. Small leaves and a wide mounded shape distinguishes *R. williamsianum* while *R. macabeanum* is recognized by its remarkably large leaves. Name stakes are placed throughout the garden to help identify noteworthy specimens.

The garden's handsome design employs many prominent features such as rock walls, beautiful wooden bridges, the Paddison Fountain (named for volunteer Fred Paddison), charming waterfalls, and thirteen natural springs to further enhance the landscape. Perennials, bulbs, and other companion plantings add seasonal interest and variety, while a wealth of trees—magnolias, maples, and rare varieties—complement the rhododendron collections.

An urban sanctuary with inherent natural beauty, Crystal Springs shelters examples of bald cypress (a deciduous conifer native to the southeastern United States) as well as a deciduous dawn redwood grown from seed acquired in 1947 from the Arnold Arboretum in Boston. In late winter look for the unusual cornelian cherry dogwood, which displays yellow flowers and interesting peeling bark.

One of the newer garden sections, the wetland area (funded by the Portland Garden Club), incorporates plants and grasses that thrive in boggy conditions. A flourishing duck population and birdlife bring another element of charm to the setting. Herons, wild geese, and unusual species of waterfowl are often sighted, to the delight of bird-watchers and garden visitors.

The Overlook area provides excellent views of the garden. Take advantage of the benches and enjoy one of Portland's most convenient garden settings.

❀ **Admission:** Free Labor Day through February. Fee charged March through Labor Day, Thursday through Monday 10:00 A.M. to 6:00 P.M. **Garden open:** Daily dawn to dusk.
Further information: Plan your visit for the first Saturday in April and enjoy a fine display of early bloomers. See the Web site for more details. The garden is wheelchair accessible.

Directions: The garden is located in Portland's Eastmoreland neighborhood, 1 block north of Woodstock Boulevard, and situated between Eastmoreland Golf Course and Reed College. Public transit information and directions are found on the Web site.

3. Elk Rock, the Garden at the Bishop's Close

11800 Southwest Military Lane, **Portland,** OR 97219;
(503) 636–5613, (800) 452–2562; www.diocese-oregon.org

*E*NVISION a serene cliffside setting high above the Willamette River. Enchanting Elk Rock garden is situated on property purchased in the early 1890s by Peter and Thomas Kerr, together with their partner, Patrick Gifford. Created over time by Mr. and Mrs. Peter Kerr, the Elk Rock garden was presented as a gift to the Episcopal Bishop of Oregon in 1957. The Elk Rock Garden Committee has supervised the garden since 1986, continuing to maintain the landscape as a peaceful retreat of outstanding beauty.

An important representation of Northwest garden design, Elk Rock encompasses approximately six acres. The formal garden plan incorporates a series of separate, stylized rooms surrounding the Scottish manor-style house built for Mr. and Mrs. Kerr. John Olmsted was called upon to site the house and is responsible for its inviting views of Mount Hood.

Ornamented throughout the seasons with an exceptional collection of magnolias, the Elk Rock garden features a bounteous assortment of unusual shrubs and trees, flourishing perennials, and prominent displays of bulbs. At the visitor center, pick up a pamphlet for a self-guided tour of the landscape.

March is known as "Magnolia month" at Elk Rock, where species and varieties of that lustrous genus of trees thrive in Portland's climate. During March the garden's thirty-five uncommonly diverse magnolia specimens offer a grand floral exhibition.

Begin your Elk Rock tour near the residence. Follow the paths around the house and chapel areas, where a number of established magnolia trees are found. Look also for such other noteworthy specimens as the winter-blooming silktassel, the summer-blooming golden rain tree, and a fine example of ornamental kiwi vine (*Actinidia kolomikta*). Vigorous and highly decorative, this climber bears extravagant foliage distinguished by heart-shaped leaves splashed with cream and flushes of deep pink.

Proceed along the Cliff Cottage Walk, where you'll discover madrone, stewartia, and Sitka spruce trees. Here the fragrant sarcococca shrub (*Sarcococca ruscifolia*) delights winter visitors with its aromatic proclamation. Explore the Spring Walk, with colorful bulbs interspersed throughout the perennials, and inhale the delicious scents of a host of viburnums blooming from January through April. Don't miss another seasonal highlight—the sweeping vistas of the garden's elegant lawns carpeted in crocuses from January through April.

Dedicated to Thomas Kerr, the garden's Cascades section is characterized by a fine assemblage of trees featuring a wondrous range of textural bark. The Franklin tree (*Franklinia alatamaha*), a rare variety of birch, and the snakebark maple are selected landmarks. Flowering displays of winterhazels accentuate the arboreal plantings, while shrubs such as camellias, daphnes, fothergillas, hebes, and rhododendrons add noteworthy beauty throughout the seasons.

Investigate the Point, which offers stirring views of the Willamette River. For a tranquil interlude, enjoy the restored Rock Garden. These are just two aspects of Elk Rock that I recall fondly from my last visit. At Elk Rock, limited parking seems to keep the crowds away, making the Garden at the Bishop's Close a peaceful haven.

Garden lovers who have discovered Elk Rock's verdant greenery and memorable groves of trees, however, return again and again. I recommend placing Elk Rock, the Garden at the Bishop's Close, prominently on your itinerary of Portland-area gardens. Having contemplated the restrained yet picturesque landscape, I can vouch for the garden's uplifting atmosphere.

❀ **Admission:** Free; donations are encouraged.

Garden open: Daily 8:00 A.M. to 5:00 P.M.; closed some holidays.

Further information: Group visits are by appointment only. Call before visiting to confirm hours. Wheelchair access is limited; there are no public restrooms.

Directions: The garden is located in the vicinity of Lake Oswego and the Sellwood Bridge. Take Highway 43 south from downtown Portland to Southwest Military Road and turn left toward the river, then right onto Southwest Military Lane. You may phone for more detailed directions.

4. The Grotto

The National Sanctuary of Our Sorrowful Mother, Northeast
Eighty-fifth Avenue and Sandy Boulevard, **Portland,** OR (mailing
address: P.O. Box 20008, Portland, OR 97294); (503) 254–7371;
www.thegrotto.org

A SIXTY-TWO-ACRE retreat with towering fir trees and a
wealth of native flora, the Grotto features a rock cave
carved into the base of a 110-foot cliff wall. A marble replica of
Michelangelo's *Pieta* serves as the shrine's central focus.

Visitors may take a ten-story elevator ride to the top of the bluff
for sweeping views of the surrounding mountains and the Columbia
River Valley. To enjoy the upper level's garden setting, stroll through
the rose garden and the Marguerite M. Casey Peace Garden, which
features streams, reflection ponds, and an exultant springtime display of blooming rhododendrons.

❀ **Admission:** Free for plaza level garden except during special events;
modest fee for ride to upper level.

Garden open: Daily 9:00 A.M. to 7:30 P.M. Mother's Day through Labor
Day; hours change in fall and winter. Closed Thanksgiving and Christmas Day. The gift shop opens daily at 9:00 A.M.; call (503) 261–2424
for closing times.

Further information: Look on the Web site to learn about the history
of the Grotto, to see a listing of special events, a mass schedule, or seasonal closing hours. Call before visiting for information on wheelchair
access.

Directions: The Grotto is located ½ mile west of Interstate 205, near
the junction of Interstate 84 and I–205. You'll find a map, detailed driving directions, and public transit information on the Web site. Ample
free parking is provided.

5. Hogan and Sanderson Garden

2700/2800 block of Northeast Eleventh Avenue, **Portland,** OR
97212; (503) 621–2233 (Cistus Nursery); www.cistus.com

$\mathcal{E}$XCITING gardening endeavors are taking place in a vital Portland neighborhood, where two exceptional plantsmen—designer and author Sean Hogan and Parker Sanderson (proprietors of Cistus Nursery; see the gardenwalk entry)—have become catalysts for a flurry of horticultural activity on the 2700/2800 block of Northeast Eleventh Avenue.

To date, the unique energy is indicated by a bevy of homes boasting thriving gardens that form richly textured visual links within the community. Stroll along this expanse of Northeast Eleventh and admire alluring parkway plantings and front gardens bursting with eye-catching collections of trees, shrubs, and perennials.

Coming upon the garden created by Sean and Parker, I admired species within the plant family known as eucalypts combined stunningly with Mediterranean specimens.

Rare plants abound, with more provocative specimens than it seems possible to take in at one time. Leaf textures, in particular, exhibit a range of velvety and felted surfaces, emerging in a composition dominated by a silvery theme. A choice jasmine with narrow, pearly foliage and sweetly scented blooms stands out. In springtime the unusual square-shaped flowers of *Philadelphus mexicanus*

Exploring Historic Irvington

Visiting the Hogan and Sanderson Garden in Portland's historic Irvington neighborhood? If so, you may want to amble over to Northeast Fremont Street between Northeast Thirteenth and Fifteenth Avenues, where you'll find shops and restaurants. Or explore a hub of activity on Northeast Broadway Street.

'Rosemary Brown' are a conspicuous asset, set off by the gleaming undersides of its leaves.

Callistemon pallidus, a patio-size bottlebrush clothed in chartreuse flowers, creates a fine display, while fragrant *Osmanthus fragrans* var. *thunbergii* draws garden visitors with its maroon new growth and pale orange flowers.

In a section dubbed the Moon Garden, the magnificent canes of the Chinese species rose (*Rosa sericea* var. *pteracantha*), stretch upward and outward, displaying translucent red thorns that positively glow when backlit by the setting sun.

Look for the enormous, deeply lobed leaves of *Tetrapanax papyrifer* 'Steroidal Giant'. This towering variety of the rice paper plant is the sort of surprising sight that appears wherever your gaze might momentarily settle amid the plentiful flora.

Seasonal container plantings add another level of interest to the rarified evergreens gathered together in the Hogan and Sanderson Garden. Formidable leaves accented by red margins give a lushly tropical appearance to the Abyssinian banana, *Ensete ventricosum rubra*.

During my tour of the garden, I noticed a collection of solanum species potted up (perhaps to keep them from attacking!). Indeed, the array of outrageous forms and textures stopped me in my tracks.

Solanum marginatum displays prominent spikes down the center of its leaves and along the length of its veins. Each entrancing leaf possesses splendidly frosted, curled edges as well. Equally sinister and exotic, *S. pyracanthum* is cloaked in shapely blue-green leaves animated by forbidding yet decorative tangerine thorns.

❀ **Admission:** Free.

    Garden open: Daily during daylight hours.

    Further information: Sidewalks are wheelchair accessible.

    Directions: Located in Portland's historic Irvington neighborhood, bordered on the north by Northeast Fremont Street from Northeast Seventh Avenue to Northeast Twenty-sixth Avenue, and Northeast Broadway to the south; about ten minutes from downtown Portland by car. Go to www.trimet.org for public transportation information.

6. Ira C. Keller Memorial Fountain Park

Southwest Third Avenue between Market and Clay Streets,
Portland, OR 97204; (503) 823–7529 (Portland Parks and
Recreation); www.portlandparks.org

*T*HE IRA C. KELLER FOUNTAIN completed in 1971 emerges as the stunning centerpiece of this downtown Portland city park space.

From its site facing the Keller Auditorium, the popular gathering spot known as Ira's Fountain (or Civic Theater Forecourt) features a design by Angela Danadjieva for Lawrence Halprin Associates. The exuberant water feature is composed of streams amid a terrace shaded by trees. The flowing water narrows then converges in a series of formidable waterfalls. A city landmark to seek out.

❀ **Admission:** Free.

    Garden open: Daily 5:00 A.M. to midnight.

    Further information: Call Portland Parks and Recreation or visit the Web site to learn more. A sidewalk around the fountain provides some wheelchair access.

Directions: The park is located in the heart of downtown, about 3 blocks west of Southwest Front Avenue and the Willamette River.

7. Leach Botanical Garden

6704 Southeast 122nd Avenue, **Portland,** OR 97236;
(503) 823-9503; www.portlandparks.org

*T*HE TRANQUIL setting of Leach Botanical Garden was once home to botanist Lilla Leach and her husband, John. Some four decades after the Leaches built their colonial revival–style manor house and first established this lovely five-acre garden, the couple donated the house and the surrounding property to the city of Portland in 1979. According to the terms of their bequest, the Leach Garden became the city's first public botanical garden when it opened in 1981.

Currently the garden occupies a nine-acre parcel of land operated by a group of fervent volunteers, known as the Leach Garden Friends, in cooperation with Portland Parks and Recreation. The lovely landscape features 1½ miles of trails emphasizing Northwest native plants.

Explore the garden's established plant collections and you will become acquainted with plants Lilla Leach herself discovered. Among the most notable species associated with Mrs. Leach are plants such as *Kalmiopsis leachiana*, which resembles a small rhododendron, and a native iris, *Iris innominata*. You can refer to the self-guiding nature trail map to select among the garden's informative and pleasurable walks. You'll enjoy display gardens and an existing native woodland where the Leaches integrated vast arrays of appealing plants.

Combining unspoiled areas of both moist and dry coniferous woods; streamside plantings; and fern, rock, and bog gardens, the Leach Botanical Garden puts visitors in touch with the varied habitats of the pristine Pacific Northwest. One thousand five hundred plant species carry labels, in keeping with the garden's educational aims and community outreach.

A highlight of the garden is the Leach Collection, which offers wonderful displays throughout the year. Arranged and planted so that different species of plants in the same genus coexist, this area presents a unique opportunity to compare related witch hazels, hollies, hellebores, and viburnums as well as hybrid rhododendrons and southeast azaleas. The outstanding plants in this collection exhibit lovely leaf color, aromatic bloom, ornamental berries, and sculptured branches.

Even during a summer visit, one can't help but notice the generous foliage of the garden's fine collection of trilliums lining the edges of woodland paths. I encourage you to visit in mid- to late March, however, to witness the sight of these magical wildflowers in bloom. They light up the garden's woods! The Leach Botanical Garden's trillium collection includes *Trillium albidum*, with its exceptionally delicate white flower; *T. Kurabayashi*, a very large species with deep maroon flowers; *T. parviflorum*, native to the Portland area (and easily confused with *T. albidum*); and an exciting addition and recently named strain, *T. ovatum* 'Barbara Welsh'.

❀ **Admission:** Free.

Garden open: Tuesday through Saturday 9:00 A.M. to 4:00 P.M., Sunday 1:00 to 4:00 P.M.; closed Monday and some holidays. The gift shop is open during garden hours.

Further information: The gift shop carries a fine sampling of garden items. Look for a schedule of events, classes, plant sales, and tour information on the Web site. Call before visiting to confirm hours or to hear about English teas taking place in the manor house. There is wheelchair access to the manor house, front display gardens, parking, and restrooms.

Directions: Located in the Pleasant Valley neighborhood of Southeast Portland, 4 blocks south of Southeast 122nd Avenue and 3 miles east of the Foster Road Exit. Follow I–205 south to the Foster Road exit, then go east on Foster Road to Southeast 122nd Avenue. Detailed driving directions and public transit information are on the Web site.

8. Peninsula Park Rose Garden

North Ainsworth Street and Albina Avenue, **Portland,** OR 97217; (503) 823–7529 (Portland Parks and Recreation); www.portlandparks.org

A REQUIRED stopover on your garden forays in the rose capital, the seventeen-acre municipal Peninsula Park contains one of Portland's most beloved gardens, the Peninsula Park Rose Garden. The formal setting boasts manicured boxwood hedges that function effectively as structural elements, at once containing and complementing the luxuriant roses on exhibit.

Presenting a radiant blend of plants and hardscaping, the Peninsula Park Rose Garden showcases nearly 9,000 roses cared for by personnel from Portland Parks and Recreation as well as local volunteers from the community.

Traditional yet imaginative, the park's sunken-garden plan features a tapestry of color and fragrance within a symmetrical framework. Once the site of patriotic gatherings during the World War I era, the park has a prominently positioned octagonal bandstand dating from that time. Its grand scale, ornate tile roof, and decorative metalwork remind visitors of Portland's past and our nation's erstwhile history. From a design standpoint, today the bandstand takes on the appearance of a spectacular gazebo. It's the perfect place from which to view grassy pathways that weave their way like cushiony ribbons through the maze of heavenly scented rosebushes.

Much less visited than the Washington Park Rose Garden, the Peninsula Park Rose Garden is recognized as one of the city's hidden treasures. Here spectacular blooms emerge in late May and early June and continue well into October. Another distinctive characteristic of the garden is its glassy pool. Centrally placed in the midst of the garden's compelling geometry, the water feature incorporates a soothing fountain that adds a note of calm to the surroundings.

Plan to linger among the opulent blooms cultivated at the Peninsula Park Rose Garden. Be on the lookout for Portland's official rose, 'Mme. Caroline Testout'. First bred in France in 1890, the rose's impressive pedigree was established in the days when countless bushes of this type were planted throughout the town, earning Portland its illustrious designation as the City of Roses!

Admission: Free.

Garden open: Daily from dawn to dusk.

Further information: Donations are welcomed and may be deposited in the donation boxes in the garden. The garden has some stairs and gravel paths; wheelchair access is limited.

Directions: Located in North Portland's Piedmont neighborhood, the garden is on the south boundary of Peninsula Park. Take Interstate 5 to the Portland Boulevard exit, and go east to Albina, then turn right. Call Portland Parks and Recreation for detailed directions.

9. Portland Classical Chinese Garden

Northwest Third Avenue and Everett Street, **Portland,** OR
(mailing address: P.O. Box 3706, Portland, OR 97208);
(503) 228–8131; www.portlandchinesegarden.org

*E*NCHANTINGLY named Garden of Awakening Orchids, or Lan Su Yuan, the Portland Classical Chinese Garden finds inspiration in the classical urban gardens of Suzhou—China's garden city and Portland's sister city in China.

The garden is an authentically built classical scholar's garden of the Ming dynasty. In June 1999 groundbreaking for the walled garden took place, and since opening in September 2000, the garden has received an enthusiastic welcome from the public along with kudos from the media.

Magnificent structures and a beguiling overall landscape distinguish this classical Chinese garden, the first of its kind in the United States. Artists and expert artisans from Suzhou made up the garden's design team, who later traveled to Portland to assemble the prefabricated buildings and create decorative elements like stonework boasting an incredible attention to detail.

Stout stone lions stand sentry as you approach the garden's main portal. Pass through the inscribed gate framing the entryway and step inside to find a lovely lake, functioning as a harmonious link between each aspect of the garden. Notice the "Three Friends of Winter," a complementary grouping of a pine, graceful bamboo, and a plum tree that traditionally appear in Chinese art. Within this planting a Lake Tai rock holds a prominent place. As you proceed to discover the garden in its full beauty, the symbolic nature of such distinctive rocks is revealed as integral to the philosophical character of the idealized setting.

Wander through the garden and you'll come upon terraces poised to look out over a pond adorned with water lilies. Elsewhere a rockery and waterfall create a commanding tableau.

Aesthetic features are numerous: spacious pavilions with tile roofs, covered bridges, craggy limestone rocks representing cloud configurations, and mesmerizing mosaics.

Around every turn a unique view emerges, taking in intimate vignettes from a "crab-apple blossom" mosaic stone pattern underfoot to an illustrious carved panel that draws you in at eye level. Sheltered within the Knowing the Fish Pavilion, you'll perceive vistas designed to appear distant, from the Clouds Bridge and Locking the Moon Pavilion to the Tower of Cosmic Reflections.

Amid the garden's emblematic mountains and stirring water features, plants artfully accompany the architecture. Plants sourced in the Pacific Northwest include species indigenous to China. Pomegranate, peach, osmanthus, Chinese paper bush (*Edgeworthia chrysantha*), and magnolia arise as alluring accents surrounding the Hall of Brocade Clouds. In the courtyard outside the Scholar's Study—the Celestial Hall of Permeating Fragrance—the perfume of gardenias and wintersweet lingers on the air.

Banana trees with broad leaves grow below the roof tiles in the Scholar's Courtyard, where specially designed drip tiles produce a calculated effect: beads of water create a melodious sound when raindrops fall.

Seek out the two-story Tea House for a refreshing respite from your amble around the garden as well as for delightful views. Your retreat from the sounds of the surrounding neighborhood to the reflective atmosphere of the Portland Classical Chinese Garden promises a multitude of enthralling sensory and seasonal pleasures on-view year-round.

❄ **Admission:** Fee.

Garden open: Daily 9:00 A.M. to 6:00 P.M. from April through October; daily 10:00 A.M. to 5:00 P.M. from November through March. Closed Thanksgiving, Christmas, and New Year's Day. The gift shop and teahouse are open during garden hours; last sitting for the teahouse is a half hour before closing.

Further information: Look on the Web site for a wealth of information about the garden (a self-sustaining, nonprofit organization funded by donors, members, and visitors). Tours generally take place daily at noon and 1:00 P.M.; no reservation is required. Phone the main number in advance and dial extension 0 to confirm tour times for the day of your visit. Call or log on to the Web site before visiting to learn about special programs, performances, demonstrations, and exhibits. An ADA-wheelchair-accessible route allows travel throughout the garden.

Directions: The Classical Chinese Garden occupies the Portland city block bounded by Northwest Everett and Flanders Streets and Northwest Second and Third Avenues in the city's Old Town/Chinatown neighborhood. To reach the garden, take I–405 to the Everett Street exit and turn east. A map and public transit information for travel by bus or the light-rail system is available on the Web site.

10. Washington Park

Head of Southwest Park Place, **Portland,** OR 97210;
(503) 823–7529 (Portland Parks and Recreation);
www.portlandparks.org

*I*F A GARDEN traveler possesses the stamina, an entire day could easily be devoted to investigating the green spaces of Washington Park and its acclaimed International Rose Test Garden, Japanese Gardens, and Hoyt Arboretum.

John Olmsted helped improve Washington Park back in 1903 when he suggested the separation of pedestrian traffic from vehicle roadways, as well as other changes. The park also boasts natural areas and picnic facilities, a children's playground, tennis court, and the Washington Park Zoo.

Linked to Washington Park is Forest Park, a 5,000-acre woodland wonderland. Reigning as the largest municipal park in the United States, Portland's Forest Park offers access to miles and miles of rustic nature trails for hiking, biking, or running.

❀ **Admission:** Free.
Garden open: Daily 5:00 A.M. to midnight.
Further information: Wheelchair accessibility is limited.
Directions: The park is located west of downtown Portland. Take West Burnside Avenue and follow signs to the park. The TriMet bus #63 provides service to Washington Park and its gardens.

11. Washington Park's Hoyt Arboretum

4000 Southwest Fairview Boulevard, **Portland**, OR 97221;
(503) 865–8733; www.hoytarboretum.org

*M*ORE THAN 900 species of trees and shrubs thrive in the invigorating oasis of Portland's Hoyt Arboretum. A handsome, recently constructed visitor center is the result of a successful partnership between the experienced staff of the Portland Parks and Recreation Department and the spirited membership of Hoyt Arboretum Friends Foundation. The center represents the energy and commitment of the arboretum's administration.

Equip yourself with a trail map, then proceed to explore the extensive system of trails meandering through the arboretum's 175 acres. Located on an elevated crest not far from the city's downtown neighborhood, the Hoyt Arboretum introduces garden and nature lovers to a forested retreat with wonderful views of one of the Pacific Northwest's most agreeable cities.

Encircled by native firs and cedars, Hoyt Arboretum's 10 miles of trails are planted with exciting and diverse arboreal specimens. Labels on trees point out Hoyt's exceptional collections of conifers, heavenly scented magnolias, dogwoods, oaks, and maples. Be sure to investigate the Bristlecone Pine Trail. Look, too, for examples of the rare Brewer's weeping spruce.

A gardenwalk at the Hoyt Arboretum will help you understand Portland's reputation as a celebrated horticultural capital.

❀ **Admission:** Free.

Garden open: Daily 6:00 A.M. to 10:00 P.M. The visitor center is open daily 9:00 A.M. to 4:00 P.M.

Further information: Visit the Web site or call the visitor center to learn about free guided tours scheduled on weekends from April through October at the arboretum. Tours begin at 2:00 P.M.; they are drop-in and held rain or shine. Seasonal tours offer themed walks like Fall Color, Flowering Trees, and Spring Wildflowers. Most trails are unpaved; however, the visitor center, its restrooms, and 2 miles of trails are wheelchair accessible.

Directions: The arboretum is about 2 miles west of downtown Portland. The TriMet bus #63 stops directly in front of the visitor center. Or ride the Westside Light Rail line and get off at the Washington Park Zoo stop. Walk uphill from there to the visitor center. Detailed driving directions and a map of the arboretum can be found on the Web site.

12. Washington Park's International Rose Test Garden

400 Southwest Kingston Avenue, **Portland,** Oregon, 97201;
(503) 823–3636; www.portlandparks.org, www.rosegardenstore.org

$\mathcal{R}$OSE LOVERS flock to Portland rose gardens around mid-June, when the queen of all flowers generally reaches peak bloom in the City of Roses. The Peninsula Park Rose Garden (see the separate gardenwalk entry) deserves a visit, as does Portland's sublime four-and-a-half-acre International Rose Test Garden.

Located near the entrance to Washington Park off West Burnside Boulevard, the International Rose Test Garden holds claim to being the oldest test garden in the United States. Established in 1917, this rose lover's paradise showcases more than 8,000 roses representing over 525 varieties.

The garden's design employs a medley of structural supports to artistically display the countless roses. These underpinnings create intriguing contexts that elegantly enhance the abundantly planted, terraced beds. Taken together, the garden's tall steel arches, two-dimensional aluminum espalier structures, and three-dimensional pyramidal forms accentuate the landscaping's distinctive levels.

As you ascend the garden's staircases and walkways, pause beneath archways wrapped in fragrant climbing roses. You'll see clipped green lawns and observe how their cool expanses bring harmony to the garden's design. As you move from one level to the next, note how the arches become momentary thresholds that entreat you to stop and smell the roses! When planning a stopover, bear in mind that blooming roses continue to flourish throughout the summer months and well into October.

A special highlight of the International Rose Test Garden is the Gold Medal Garden. Celebrating fifty years of award-winning roses, the area's signs help visitors identify the prized collection on view. As you walk through this national testing ground for new roses, you'll discover rows of unfamiliar roses that have garnered awards bestowed by the city of Portland on exciting varieties not yet released to the public.

Above the Gold Medal Garden, the Royal Rosarian Garden offers beautiful views into the rose garden and the city beyond. Here, planted along the edge of a flat paved walkway, are roses selected by "prime ministers" of the Royal Rosarians—an official Portland group of greeters. Reigning for one year, individual prime ministers select a special rose that is then installed in a sequential planting. The roses displayed in this highly accessible garden area can be readily enjoyed by visitors with limited mobility.

Individual gardens within the Rose Test Garden include a pastoral outdoor amphitheater with inviting seating upholstered in green grass. The arrangement of fastidiously maintained rose beds contains an area known as the Queen's Walk, featuring plaques that recognize every Queen of Rosaria since the early part of the century.

Enjoy a quiet reprieve from your hectic itinerary within the confines of the Shakespeare Garden, situated in the southeast section of the garden. You'll come upon graceful paved paths of red brick, perennial plantings, and varieties of roses selected for their evident association with England's foremost bard. These include 'Sweet Juliet' and 'Climbing Ophelia'.

At the garden's upper level, don't miss the Beach Memorial Fountain, designed by Lee Kelley. This contemporary construction, erected in 1974, honors Frank E. Beach, the gentleman responsible for coining Portland's motto, City of Roses. Look for the stunning contrast between the gleaming stainless-steel form and the aged patina of nearby moss-covered rock walls, elegantly draped in lavish cascades of delicate, pale white roses.

From the rose garden, you have a much-photographed view of downtown Portland and Mount Hood. May through August are generally considered peak viewing times, as these are the months when clear blue skies are most likely to reveal terrific vistas that can reach as far as Mount St. Helens. Glorious views aside, you'll surely enjoy a visit to the garden whenever you happen to plan a jaunt through Portland. Note that roses are in bloom continuously from late May to early June for the earliest bloomers, and through mid-October for the later ones.

❀ **Admission:** Free.

Garden open: Daily 7:30 A.M. to 9:00 P.M. The Rose Garden Store is open daily at 10:00 A.M.; call (503) 227–7033 for closing hours.

Further information: Donations are welcomed and may be deposited in the donation boxes in the garden. Visit www.rosegardenstore.org for Rose Garden Store hours, to enjoy a trove of rose-related lore, or to shop online for gift items with a rose theme. Wheelchair access to the rose garden is limited: A ramp at the south end of the parking lot goes down one side of the garden, allowing a part of the garden to be viewed.

Directions: Located west of downtown in Washington Park. Take the zoo exit off Highway 26, then follow the signs leading to the International Rose Test Garden. To see detailed directions for driving, walking, or public transportation, or to download a map, go to www.rosegardenstore.org. The Rose Garden Store is located at 850 Southwest Rose Garden Way, at the top of the International Rose Test Garden and south of the parking area.

13. Washington Park's Japanese Garden

611 Southwest Kingston Avenue, **Portland**, OR 97201;
(503) 223–1321; www.japanesegarden.com

*P*ORTLAND'S lovely Japanese Garden is located just above the International Rose Test Garden in Washington Park. Opened to the public in 1967, this popular five-and-a-half-acre garden was designed by Professor Takuma Tono. To discover the intrinsic beauty of the garden's five distinctive garden styles, devote adequate time to each of the five areas: the Strolling Pond Garden, the Tea Garden, the Natural Garden, the Sand and Stone Garden, and the Flat Garden.

As you pass under the wisteria-draped arbor, the Strolling Pond Garden will be revealed. Note the rough beauty of the weathered stones at the arbor's base. These aged stones provide a striking contrast to the wisteria's generous flowers and the vine's extravagant foliage. Diverse elements such as plants and rocks are typically used to heighten one's perception of the garden's aesthetic qualities and to invoke the mindful resonance associated with Japanese gardens.

The arbor's portal functions as a frame, revealing one of the garden's stone lanterns. Presented as a gift to the city of Portland by its sister city in Japan, Sapporo, the multitiered, 18-foot-high traditional pagoda tower appears unexpectedly as you walk through the arbor. The idea of a hidden view like this one embodies an essential aspect of Japanese garden design. The largest of the five gardens, the Strolling Pond Garden, presents a succession of lovely vignettes, many of which are accentuated by water features. Water is in fact one of the most significant elements of the garden's overall plan.

In a Japanese garden, the idea of change—day turning into night and the seasons passing—can be demonstrated by a single, transitory experience. During one visit here, I noted how a shifting ray of sunlight created glimmering highlights on the russet leaves of a cut-leaf maple. Behind the tree, the rebuilt waterfall known as the "heavenly falls" was subtly enhanced by this fleeting play of light. If one takes time to perceive such ephemeral scenes, moments of perfect quietude will be the reward.

Japanese garden design reveals an infinite number of engaging perspectives throughout the seasons. Opposite the waterfall, the site becomes a springtime haven when a grove of trees produces a sparkling exhibition of cherry blossoms. Enjoy a silent ramble in any corner of the garden; it will gladden the heart and uplift the spirit.

Careful tending of the varied garden settings is readily apparent in the meticulous condition of the plantings, in the artistic charac-ter of such man-made components as bamboo fencing bound with twine, and in the craftsmanship of the garden's buildings. You'll also find crane sculptures and the authentic Moon Bridge crossing the garden's upper pond. To the south, you'll encounter a creek and the lower pond. Look for the beautifully crafted Zig Zag Bridge to take you through iris beds. A stimulating visual confluence of blues, pur-ples, and white materializes in these beds around the third week in June. The lower pond features stones symbolizing the tortoise and the crane; both creatures represent longevity.

Passing a smaller waterfall, note the precisely placed plantings of Japanese maples, the sculptural presence of stones, and the sounds of falling water. Observe the purity of the natural world in the grace-ful asymmetry of the weeping tree forms or the low-growing ferns enhancing the edges of rocky hillsides. Together these elements create a harmonious, tranquil mood.

In contrast the Sand and Stone Garden presents a walled space where the abstract patterns of raked sand and weathered stone can be contemplated. An overlook provides fine views of this pristine retreat, but in order to experience the garden's solitary, spiritual center, you must descend a series of steep stone steps and sit and reflect on the forms placed here to suggest the sea and the Buddha's sacrifice.

Near the overlook is a hidden alcove offering a bench set under the cover of trees. This private place of meditation presents a fine vantage point from which to observe the textures of lichens layered over rough rocks, to gaze out upon the hilly terrain, or to listen to the sounds of a rushing stream. Walk a bit farther and you'll arrive at the pavilion's rustic deck, where a gleaming cityscape lies sprawling in the distance.

These are but a handful of impressions of Portland's Japanese Garden, where garden travelers delight in an exquisite landscape representing the venerable influences of age-old religions and the aesthetic concepts integral to Japan's cultural heritage.

❉ **Admission:** Fee.

Garden open: Monday noon to 7:00 P.M., Tuesday through Sunday 10:00 A.M. to 7:00 P.M., from April through September; Monday noon to 4:00 P.M., Tuesday through Sunday 10:00 A.M. to 4:00 P.M., from October through March 31. Last admission is a half hour before closing time. Closed Thanksgiving, Christmas, and New Year's Day.

Further information: Call the gift shop at (503) 223–5055 to confirm hours or to learn about daily guided tours offered during April through October. Garden paths include hilly areas, uneven steps and gravel walkways: Call ahead to discuss wheelchair-accessible routes, or look for the accessibility feature on the Web site, where you'll find a full explanation of wheelchair access in the garden.

Directions: The Japanese Garden is located in Washington Park, in the west hills of Portland. Travel west on Burnside Street from downtown, past Northwest Twenty-third Avenue; turn left onto Tichner, then right onto Kingston Avenue. You'll find public transit information and detailed driving directions on the Web site.

14. Cistus Nursery

22711 Northwest Gillihan Road, **Sauvie Island,** OR 97231;
(503) 621–2233 (nursery), (503) 282–7706 (office); www.cistus.com

A SOJOURN to Cistus Nursery on bucolic Sauvie Island will refresh your spirits when you feel like taking a break from a tour of bustling Portland.

Travel fifteen minutes north of the city and cross the Sauvie Island Bridge, and you come upon a peaceful landscape encompassing a savannah punctuated by old oaks and a view of Mount St. Helens. Continue along Gillihan Road, making your way to Cistus, and you'll pass growers of organic vegetables, cut flowers, and herbs.

Sean Hogan, author of horticultural reference works including the definitive *Flora*, created this destination nursery with his partner, Parker Sanderson. All-round shining lights in the Portland gardening scene, Hogan and Sanderson have designed a series of lush display gardens illustrating the fine art of uniting plants in compelling combinations. Visitors can also learn a great deal from botanical arrangements that feature wide-ranging plant material.

The visual impact is immediate and striking, beginning when you take in deep borders lining the long drive leading to the parking area. The Mediterranean section on the right presents a multitude of western native plants intermingled with varieties from other dry-summer regions. You can look to these plantings to feature selections that receive no summer irrigation.

A glorious presentation arises directly opposite, where silvery tones and blue foliage combine in a lovely alliance. Facing west, this

The Hardy Plant Society of Oregon

Dedicated to the study, use, and promotion of hardy herbaceous perennial plants—yet encompassing a greater realm of gardening interests—the Hardy Plant Society of Oregon (HPSO) is a high-energy group without rival, and one that merits your consideration for membership.

A nonprofit organization run by volunteers, the HPSO focuses on the Pacific Northwest area, where it offers terrific benefits to its members. Excellent reasons to join include stimulating monthly newsletters; garden tours; discount-priced horticultural books; plant sales; and, in particular, exciting, high-caliber programs.

Published twice a year, the *Bulletin* contains horticultural articles, book reviews, and other interesting items—all contributed by members. On various garden tours, members have sojourned to the south of England, Scotland, Ireland, and the Cote d'Azur. As I write this entry, a journey to Tuscany looms on the horizon.

Plant sales held in April and September each year offer dazzling panoplies of perennials, trees, and shrubs marketed by some seventy to eighty specialty growers.

The HPSO has a user-friendly Web site (www.hardyplant society.org) that lets you navigate among links of interest to gardeners, from top-notch gardens and botanical societies to educational sites, nurseries, and other hardy plant groups. Check the Web site's home page for notices of upcoming lectures, workshops, and special events. Or click on the calendar, where a recent talk by acclaimed writer Michael Pollan was a highlight. You can also contact them by mail (1930 Northwest Lovejoy Street, Portland, OR 97209) or by phone (503–224–5718).

Whatever your level of gardening expertise, you will find that the Hardy Plant Society of Oregon can be counted on to provide enlightening, entertaining, and provocative activities and meetings.

section takes full advantage of dramatic backlighting when the sun dips down.

The nursery draws attention to geographical collections, too, exemplified by an arrangement of companionable New Zealand species. You'll also discover structured displays of tropicals that emphasize exciting plant possibilities, and color associations take center stage in themed borders.

Hogan is knowledgeable as well as enthusiastic about broad-leaved evergreens. Head north of the retail area and seek out the mesic environment, which requires some irrigation. Highlighted here are exceptional oak, magnolia, and schefflera specimens.

One of the most commanding sights emerges in the entrance garden, where euphorbias, variegated yuccas, agaves, grasses, palms, and cacti come together in communities of flora distinguished by bold juxtapositions. Observe the conspicuous melding of dusty blues, chartreuse yellows, and blackish greens. Adjacent to the courtyard, a stunning border characterized by plants with rosette forms includes a wall of succulents: Cascading, textural specimens adorn the wall's surface. All are hardy choices for the Portland area.

As you stroll the nursery grounds, be sure to explore the "Araucana" and "Zonal Denial" pavilions, where plantaholics can pick from Southern Hemisphere plants or hardy tropicals and bamboos amid the enthralling offerings.

❀ **Admission:** Free.
   Garden open: Call or look on the Web site for seasonal hours.
   Further information: Tables and chairs provided for picnicking at the nursery. The main and secondary paths are wheelchair accessible.
   Directions: Take U.S. Highway 30 (St. Helens Road) from Portland, traveling 10 miles north to the Sauvie Island Bridge, then turn left at the base of the bridge, going under it onto Gillihan Road. Drive 5½ miles to the nursery. Detailed directions and a printer-friendly map are on the Web site.

15. Joy Creek Nursery

20300 Northwest Watson Road, **Scappoose,** OR 97056;
(503) 543–7474; www.joycreek.com

$\mathcal{G}$ARDENERS in the Portland area rave about the plants offered
at Joy Creek Nursery. During a mid-June stopover, I was bowled
over by the horticultural riches and the invigorating sense of esprit
de corps I discovered at Joy Creek's thirty-nine-acre operation.

Among the nursery's delights are flourishing demonstration
gardens along with pottery and garden ornaments. The Joy Creek
test gardens feature exceedingly beautiful delphiniums bursting
forth in glorious bloom. I found rows of these flowering plants stand-
ing erect with sturdy stems and displaying a range of colors from
glistening mother-of-pearl and incandescent white to the fusions of
blue-violet and dusty rose found among towering varieties.

A primary goal at Joy Creek is to educate customers and enable
them to grow and enjoy beautiful gardens of their own. In business
for some thirteen years, Joy Creek offers four acres of landscaped
gardens, including the Four Seasons Garden of 3,200 square feet.
Half of this space is a lovely area designed by Lucy Hardiman especially for classes and special events. A rose garden designed by John
Caine and the newly completed Mediterranean Garden along the
driveway capture the attention, too.

Penstemons are one of Joy Creek's specialties. More than forty
species and cultivars of penstemons were available recently, from
outrageously showy specimens such as *Penstemon* 'Raspberry Flair'
to species like *P. barbatus*, with bright green leaves and relaxed
spikes bearing red flowers, and firecracker penstemon (*P. eatonii*),
with tubular flowers of the brightest scarlet. This is also a great
place to find exceptional clematis.

❈ **Admission:** Free.

Garden open: Daily 9:00 A.M. to 5:00 P.M. from March to October, by
appointment at other times. Call in advance to arrange a visit during
the winter.

Further information: Call to confirm hours, for directions, or for details on upcoming workshops and classes. Joy Creek offers free Sunday classes beginning in April, with authoritative speakers presenting stimulating topics for new and experienced gardeners alike. Wheelchair access is limited.

Directions: Joy Creek is approximately 18 miles north of Portland. Take US 30 to Watson Road, turning left before entering the town of Scappoose. Detailed directions and a map are on the Web site.

16. Heirloom Roses

24062 Northeast Riverside Drive, **St. Paul,** OR 97137;
(503) 538–1576; www.heirloomroses.com

*R*OSE AFICIONADOS will be eager to include Heirloom Roses in their itinerary. Here, blooming bounty emerges in the lavish display gardens of 1,500 varieties of hybrid musks and perpetuals, miniature types, shrubs, climbers, ground-covering forms, and the exceedingly lovely class known as antique or old roses.

In addition you'll discover a pergola 100 feet in length supporting fifty different rambling roses. The matchless colors of multipetaled, heavenly scented David Austin English roses are represented by well over one hundred varieties.

Among the roses on exhibit, you'll see albas, centifolias, bourbons, gallicas, and damasks, with each type accorded its own planting bed. It's an excellent system for observing and learning about the various groups.

The show at Heirloom Roses begins in May, building to peak bloom around early to mid-June. Still, the picturesque gardens remain outstanding into July, as countless old roses continue to produce their elegant flowers. Visitors arriving in fall will find roses blooming into November.

You'll also find a bevy of books for sale, along with gardening supplies, accessories, and own-root roses of exceptional quality.

❀ **Admission:** Free.

Garden open: Daily 9:00 A.M. to 4:00 P.M. from September through April; 9:00 A.M. to 5:00 P.M. from May through August. Closed Thanksgiving, Christmas, New Year's Day, and Easter.

Further information: Wheelchair access is limited.

Directions: Heirloom Roses is located 25 miles from Portland. Take I–5 south to exit 278 and go west on Ehlen Road (its name changes three times). Drive 7 miles to Highway 217, then turn right and drive 1 mile to the Champoeg crossroad. Turn left, then veer right at the fork by the dairy and drive 2 miles farther to Heirloom Roses.

17. Kaiser Permanente's Tualatin Poison Prevention Garden

19185 Southwest Ninetieth Street, **Tualatin**, OR 97062; (503) 813–4820

*T*HE KAISER PERMANENTE medical organization has created three poison prevention gardens, including the Tualatin garden, which opened in 2001 in a suburb southwest of Portland. Situated adjacent to Kaiser Permanente's medical office, the garden educates the public about the hazardous toxins that can be found in the bulbs, leaves, berries, roots, flowers, or seeds of many plants.

When you arrive, ask inside at the membership services desk for a self-guiding plant list that provides basic descriptions and helps to identify plants. The poisonous parts of favorites like iris and autumn crocus, agapanthus, pieris, and rhododendron are specified, together with symptoms of poisoning.

In the garden you'll see plants commonly grown by gardeners in the region. Both native species and cultivated varieties are on view. The plant labels indicate clearly the botanical Latin and common names in English (brochures in Spanish are also available).

The garden plan emphasizes longer-lived perennials, woody shrubs, and trees for year-round interest—from horse chestnut to hydrangea to diverse evergreens. Spring bloomers like mountain laurel enliven the garden early in the growing season. Selections with showy foliage extend the garden's beauty to fall color and winter profiles.

The *Preventing Plant Poisoning* brochure suggests plants for the home gardener to avoid, particularly if young children are around. Seek out plants not generally thought to be harmful for children's gardens in the *Landscaping for Safer Gardens* pamphlet, which highlights annuals such as snapdragon, cosmos, and zinnia and perennials like carpet bugle (*Ajuga reptans*). Indian hawthorn (*Raphiolepis*) and crape myrtle (*Lagerstroemia*) feature among the shrubs and trees.

To learn more about Kaiser Permanente's other poison prevention gardens—including one at the Rockwood Medical Office in Portland and the Salmon Creek garden in Vancouver, Washington—call Kaiser Permanente's Communications and External Affairs Department weekdays at the number listed above.

�֎ **Admission:** Free.

Garden open: Monday through Friday 8:00 A.M. to 6:00 P.M.

Further information: Tours by master gardeners are available by appointment from April through October. You can call or send an e-mail to the education program coordinator Jim Gersbach at Jim.N.Gersbach@kp.org to request a private guided tour for four or more people. The garden is fully wheelchair accessible via an all-weather concrete path.

Directions: From Portland take I–5 to the Nyberg exit (exit 289). Turn right, going west, and continue about 1 mile on Tualatin–Sherwood Road; then turn right onto Southwest Ninetieth Avenue. Go left into the first driveway. The garden is to the left of the Kaiser Permanente Medical Office.

North Willamette Valley
Gardenwalks

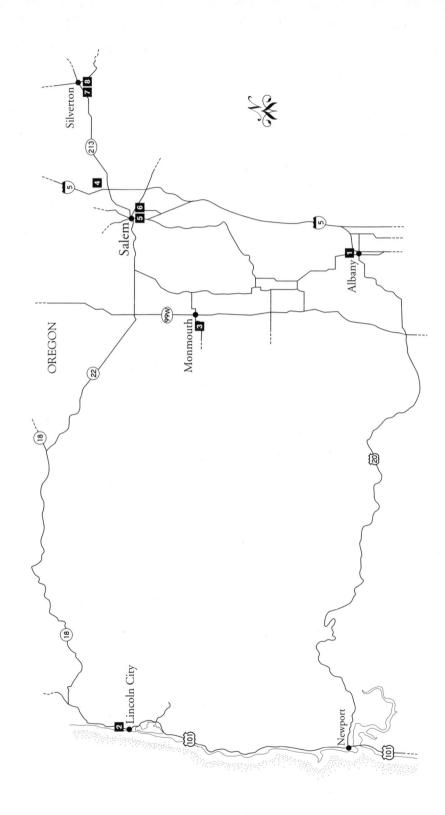

OREGON

Silverton

7 8

213

5 4

Salem

5 6

5

Albany

1

99W

Monmouth

3

22

OREGON

18

20

18

Lincoln City

2

101

Newport

101

1. Albany: Nichols Garden Nursery
2. Lincoln City: Connie Hansen Garden
3. Monmouth: Dancing Oaks Nursery
4. Salem: Adelman Peony Gardens
5. Salem: Bush's Pasture Park
6. Salem: Historic Deepwood Estate Gardens
7. Silverton: Cooley's Gardens
8. Silverton: The Oregon Garden

1. Nichols Garden Nursery

1190 Old Salem Road NE, **Albany,** OR 97321; (541) 928-9280,
(800) 422-3985; www.nicholsgardennursery.com

I WAS FIRST drawn to the Nichols Garden Nursery after glancing at its catalog and seeing the image of an inviting arbor draped lavishly in hops vine. The gateway continues to beckon visitors to enter the nursery's herb gardens, situated behind a cluster of red frame buildings.

Nichols Garden Nursery welcomes garden travelers to the Willamette Valley shop and display gardens, where ornamentals and edibles are available for purchase as well as select seeds, bulbs, roots, and plants. That original catalog photo mentioned above illustrates *Humulus lupulus*, sold as hop root cuttings. This excellent plant can be grown where seasonal coverage of a garden structure is desired. And it is but one example of Nichols's abundant offerings.

A family business specializing in herbs and rare seeds, the Nichols Garden Nursery features lovely display gardens. Proprietor Rose Marie Nichols McGee explained that the herb gardens are designed to illustrate the landscape potential of mature specimens. Among the nursery's various garden areas, "the design and plantings are done in a scale and style more reflective of what the home gardener might choose."

On a visit here you'll enjoy a parterred planting, a sweet bay hedge, a shade garden, and a flower border designed to attract bees, butterflies, and other beneficial insects. The nursery is a great place to consider the exhilarating possibilities for edible gardens. Examine ongoing vegetable trials and look at the nursery's diverse offerings of unusual vegetables and herbs, true tea plants, horseradish roots, French shallots, and gourds for use in crafts or as garden highlights.

The nursery shop's varied inventory includes spice and potpourri blends, herbal teas, gardening tools, books, and culinary ingredients such as sourdough starter and pectin.

If your travels include the Oregon Garden (see the gardenwalk entry), be sure to look for the vibrant 3,000-square-foot edible landscape display created by Nichols Garden Nursery.

❀ **Admission:** Free.

Garden open: Monday to Friday 8:00 a.m. to 5:00 p.m., Saturday 8:30 a.m. to 5:00 p.m.; closed Sunday and holidays. The shop is open during nursery hours.

Further information: Check the Web site for a listing of special events. Wheelchair access is limited; there is a ramp to enter, and gravel paths.

Directions: The nursery is located on the west side of Interstate 5, midway between exit 234 (Albany) and exit 235 (Millersburg), about 20 miles south of Salem. Look for a map on the Web site.

2. Connie Hansen Garden

1931 Northwest Thirty-third Street, **Lincoln City,** OR 97367; (541) 994-6338; www.conniehansengarden.com

*A*RTISTICALLY INCLINED as well as horticulturally gifted, botanist and avid gardener Constance Hansen moved to Lincoln City in 1973 and devoted the next twenty years to creating a lush, shady retreat.

Today the Connie Hansen Garden Conservancy lovingly maintains the one-acre landscape nestled beneath mature specimen trees,

The Scenic Route

If your starting point is either Portland or Salem, a visit to the Connie Hansen Garden in Lincoln City will (happily) involve a scenic drive through the lovely Coastal Mountain Range. Alternately, you can plan a drive along U.S. Highway 101 to explore Oregon's Central Coast, then stop over in Lincoln City to experience Connie Hansen's delightful town garden. A great garden and a scenic view—what could be better?

together with a renovated garden house where you'll find a gallery, library, gift shop, and special place devoted to ongoing classes.

Lincoln City's coastal locale contributes to the Connie Hansen Garden's moist, temperate conditions, making it a place of nurture for a host of perennials and trees. Among the treasury of plants, you'll find spectacular primroses and irises. Connie took special delight in hybridizing irises, and on the garden's southeast segment, she created the Japanese Iris Creek. In this glorious display, a graceful iris collection highlights white to purple floral color.

Around the gardening shed, maidenhair ferns are a textural contrast to the thick leaves of cyclamens. A creek runs through the garden's northern aspect, an area where in March and April you can enjoy eye-catching exhibitions of rhododendron and azalea species and hybrid varieties. Some one hundred rhododendrons grow in the garden. Look for towering *Rhododendron* 'Cynthia' near the garden house, planted decades ago by Maud Wanaker, who gardened here in the 1950s.

The garden's grassy paths weave through wonderful arrays from hellebores to heathers, with something of interest most any time of the year. Arboreal delights include dogwoods, Japanese maples, magnolias, and bevies of trees that flower in springtime.

The garden also boasts new elements, including a pond set off by water-loving plants and a rock wall on Thirty-fourth Street. Here a handsome pergola and commodious gate invite all to enter and take pleasure from a serene gardenscape.

❋ **Admission:** Free; donations welcome.

Garden open: Daily 9:00 A.M. to 5:00 P.M. The garden house is open Tuesday and Saturday 10:00 A.M. to 2:00 P.M. but is closed Saturday in December, January, and February.

Further information: Springtime plant sales, plant exchanges, a garden festival, and a Christmas open house are some of the special events you'll find listed on the Web site. Most of the garden is wheelchair accessible; the house is ADA compliant.

Directions: Lincoln City is located on the coast on U.S. Highway 101, about 2 hours west of Portland and 1 hour from Salem. From Portland take Highway 99 West to Highway 18, or from Salem take Highway 22 to Highway 18 and proceed to Lincoln City.

3. Dancing Oaks Nursery

17900 Priem Road, **Monmouth,** OR 97361; (503) 838–6058; www.dancingoaks.com

ORTICULTURE divas are spreading the word about the myriad pleasures on hand at Dancing Oaks Nursery, so it comes as no surprise that discriminating gardeners and garden lovers would extend their Willamette Valley sojourns, traveling a bit beyond the town of Monmouth to Dancing Oaks, situated in the foothills of Oregon's Coast Range Mountains.

Creators of the nursery and its eye-catching gardens, Leonard Foltz and Fred Weisensee unabashedly label themselves "unrepentant plant addicts." Their addiction results in fascinating plant combinations on exhibit in the various garden areas.

Highlights include unusual South African and South American species, the Southern Hemisphere's plant kingdom being of particular interest to the owners. The nursery's flora includes bulbs like showy alliums and calla lilies, hundreds of fine perennial and shrub varieties, trees with noteworthy foliage and flowers, and a desirable collection of vines.

Visitors are drawn to Dancing Oaks in springtime for the spirited prospect of innumerable types of bulbs in bloom, including nearly 200 different kinds of daffodils.

As the seasons progress, a split-cedar pergola some 120 feet long comes to life. Supporting vigorous 'Rambling Rector', 'Bobbie James', and other climbing roses, the structure is embellished also by clematis and choice vines such as *Akebia quinata* 'Alba'.

Along one side of the pergola's walkway, an assemblage of mock orange (*Philadelphus*) fills the air with fragrance in June. Opposite, on the walk's eastern border, a bevy of woodland specimens emerges. This intriguing display takes in perennial toad lilies, towering meadow rue, and the bold foliage of an Asian species of mayapple, *Podophyllum pleianthum*.

Seek out the rock garden to glean ideas for drought-tolerant plantings. Iris selections come into flower beginning in late February, followed by daffodil cultivars. And foxtail lilies bring high drama to the scene when their brilliant flowering spires shoot up 6 feet skyward.

The richly colorful fleshy foliage of sedums and sempervivums appears in the rockeries of the dry garden beds, together with euphorbias and achilleas. The handsome profiles of two *Eucalyptus glaucescens* are strategically placed to add impact. With silvery blue leaves and pale blue bark, these Australian trees really strike a chord with visitors.

A number of water features serve to animate the gardens. To the far right of the parking area, a naturalistic cascade of water sets the stage for carnivorous specimens, native plants, and dramatic *Gunnera tinctora*. In summer a tableau of magnificent foliage and a palette of hot flower color serves as a backdrop. Here another beautiful species of eucalyptus elevates the scenery, while the glowing leaves of golden catalpa contrast with a dark-leaved *Sambucus*, and cannas and red-hot pokers add fiery tones to the mix.

There is much more to see and to do. An area around the garden pavilion has been richly planted with rarities and adorned with urns potted up with water-loving plants. A summer garden incorporates a tropical theme that spotlights showoffs like castor bean and banana, tree dahlia and hibiscus. Close by you'll find a dryland meadow where ground-covering herbs and bulbs preen in the sun.

All sorts of enticing activities take place during the nursery's open months, spanning March through October. Expect the property to be abuzz with fun things to do, from spring open houses celebrating the bewitching blooms of hellebores to summer garden festivals and tea parties held in the pavilion. A recent schedule of workshops and classes gave participants a chance to learn how to create hypertufa troughs and gourd birdhouses or get involved in the art of casting and painting concrete leaves as garden ornamentation.

❀ **Admission:** Free.

Garden open: Wednesday through Saturday 9:30 A.M. to 5:00 P.M. from March through October. Call ahead to arrange a visit at another time or day. Open by appointment only from November 1 through the end of February.

Further information: Visit the Web site to view a portfolio of photographs, get updates on special events, or peruse the plant offerings. Wheelchair access is limited to some paths with hard surfaces; there is a handicapped parking spot and an ADA restroom.

Directions: The nursery is about 12 miles southwest of Monmouth. From the town of Monmouth, head south on Highway 99W, turning right onto Parker Road. Turn right again onto Helmick Road, and then turn left onto Elkins Road. At the end of Elkins, turn left onto Airlie Road, go ¾ mile, turn right onto Maple Grove Road. Proceed ¾ mile, turn right onto Priem Road, and continue along on this gravel road for

2 miles. Detailed driving directions from Corvallis or Salem can be found on the Web site.

4. Adelman Peony Gardens

5690 Brooklake Road NE, **Salem,** OR 97305;
(503) 393–6185; www.peonyparadise.com

*W*HO CAN RESIST the generous, many-petaled blooms and unique perfume of peonies? At Adelman Peony Gardens, you'll discover a stunning exhibition that kicks off in early May and continues through mid-June.

Adelman's production fields encompass nine acres of row upon row of full- and semidouble-type peonies, plus dramatic single blooms with large petals surrounding a vibrant center brimming with carpels and stamens.

Taken together, there are more than 300 varieties of herbaceous bush peonies and 20 varieties of intersectionals (crosses between the tree and bush peonies) growing at Adelman Gardens. The flowers bloom in luminous hues, from gossamer white to pale

Memorial Day Peonies

If you reside in a warm climate and cannot grow peonies, or simply can't fit them into your home landscape, you may want to treat yourself to a big bouquet of cut flowers, available for purchase on Memorial Day weekend at Adelman's Peony Gardens in Salem. During bloom season, visitors find vases arranged with show-stopping arrays in the indoor sales area. Outdoors, there are picnic benches and an umbrella in the field, where you can bring a lunch and savor the view—and the sweet fragrance of peony blooms.

canary yellow, and from cameo pink to candy-apple red to deep carmine. Requiring a yearly dormant period to bloom, these cold-climate plants thrive in Oregon's Willamette Valley.

In Adelman's fields you will also discover about eighty varieties of tree peonies under consideration for future sales. While my California garden does not include peonies, I have fond memories of growing them in my first garden near Chicago's lakefront. In the gemlike planting plan and lilliputian scale of that garden, I had space to grow one peony bush and one solitary tree peony. I will never forget the enchanting prospect of the tree peony in flower: After the bitter cold of wintertime, I anticipated the awakening of the garden, when springtime would herald the opening of 10-inch-wide blooms with petals like fine rose parchment paper. That these exquisite flowers adorn the woody armature of a plant barely 3 feet high makes the display an even greater pleasure.

The Adelman Gardens' catalog mentions that peonies bloom in the period after daffodils and tulips and before rhododendrons. Reminiscent of old-fashioned gardens, peonies are evocative flowers and certainly a welcome sight.

❀ **Admission:** Free.

Garden open: Daily from 9:00 A.M. to 7:00 P.M. during the annual open house (May 1 through June 15). Call to confirm dates.

Further information: Look on the Web site for a calendar of special events or call to learn more. Educational tours are available upon request during the open house. Adelman's offers peony plants in pots for sale. Grass pathways running through the fields are mainly wheelchair accessible; there are no steps. There is an accessible portable restroom here during the blooming season.

Directions: Adelman Gardens is just north of Salem. Take I–5 to exit 263 and turn east onto Brooklake Road, heading toward Brooks. Proceed 1½ miles and look for the driveway on the right. A map and directions are on the Web site.

5. Bush's Pasture Park

600 Mission Street SE, **Salem,** OR 97302; (503) 581–2228
(Salem Art Association); www.cityofsalem.net

*S*ALEM boasts a terrific, centrally located green space that beckons residents and garden travelers alike. Encompassing some ninety acres, Bush's Pasture Park was in fact a pasture at one time. The parkland's attributes include perennial borders and springtime shows of tulips and azaleas. In April a fine display of camas emerges by the tennis court.

The park's rose garden has garnered renown for its antique roses in the Tartar Old Rose Collection: Expect the blooming to peak between mid-May and mid-June. You'll want to take a break in the handsome gazebo that lends ambience to the fragrant setting.

On a stroll through the center of the park, you'll be impressed by the lofty Garry oaks. At the northwest corner of the park, there are textural plantings of select shrubs and trees, with labels provided to help you identify a particular beauty. Many bloom as early as January and February. Another attraction to explore is a Victorian greenhouse from the 1880s.

Garden open: Daily dawn to dusk. The greenhouse is open weekdays
9:00 A.M. to 4:00 P.M. and weekend afternoons.

Further information: Call the Salem Art Association for more details.
By and large the park's paths are not paved; wheelchair access is limited.

Directions: The park is in downtown Salem, directly south of Willson
Park and the state capitol. Look for a map on the Web site.

6. Historic Deepwood Estate Gardens

1116 Mission Street Southeast, **Salem**, OR 97302; (503) 363–1825;
www.deepwood.org

*T*HE GARDENS OF Historic Deepwood Estate provide a lovely
diversion when touring Oregon's capital city, and they are not
to be missed on a Willamette Valley sojourn.

You'll find an expansive landscape—nearly six acres—with
two-and-a-half acres of gardens surrounding the Historic Deepwood
Estate's 1894 Queen Anne–style house. Original stained-glass windows and oak woodwork highlight the turreted, multigabled home
designed by architect William Knighton.

Created in 1929, the formal gardens are the work of eminent designers Elizabeth Lord and Edith Schryver, who established the first
female landscape architecture enterprise in the Pacific Northwest.

A nearly 300-foot-long flower border inspired by England's
doyenne of gardening, Gertrude Jekyll, is especially interesting.
You'll find the Deepwood Estate's series of garden rooms a memorable sight throughout the year, from the impressive scale and magnificent evergreen configuration distinguishing the Great Room to
the decorative ironwork in the Scroll Garden (once known as the
Chinese Garden) and the lush flowers of the Spring Garden.

Enjoy a stroll along the nature trail, wending its way through
a woodland area of trees and wildflowers tracing Pringle Creek.

❁ **Admission:** Free.

Garden open: Daily dawn to dusk.

Further information: Call for hours and tour information for Deepwood house. Before planning a summer visit, you may also wish to call, as the gardens are reserved for weddings on many Saturdays. The majority of the gardens and the restroom are wheelchair accessible; the Deepwood house is not accessible.

Directions: Deepwood is centrally located in downtown Salem, south of the state capitol and Willamette University. A map can be viewed on the Web site. Historic Deepwood is at the east end of Bush's Pasture Park (see the previous entry).

7. Cooley's Gardens

11553 Silverton Road NE, **Silverton,** OR (mailing address:
P.O. Box 126NT, Silverton, OR 97381); (503) 873–5463;
www.cooleysgardens.com

*D*O YOUR dreams of garden visits give rise to flamboyant iris blooms? If so, you must visit Cooley's Gardens in Silverton in order to experience a real-life vision of a million or so (!) irises flouncing and strutting from mid-May to early June.

Iris growers for many decades, Cooley's is a family-operated concern and one of the largest growers worldwide. When springtime gets under way here, the tidy geometry of the display gardens— where you can enjoy up-close views of beautiful varieties—contrasts effectively with a staggering vista of the expansive growing fields. Looming beyond, the presence of Mount Hood completes the picture and inspires visitors to explore the Willamette Valley further.

Enlivening some 200 acres set aside for growing tall bearded irises, Cooley's fields bring order to beguiling rainbows of color. Iris lovers are acquainted with the language of the iris form and find the innumerable charms of the flower to be spellbinding. Fancy ruffled or fluted falls, the lacy effects and unique patterning of standards, and the vivid markings of beards are among the flower's attributes. As for floral color, the rich palette of hues that can be characteristic of one particular flower explains, perhaps, how an ardent admirer can become totally enthralled by the lavishness of iris hybrids.

Plan a stopover during Cooley's annual Anniversary Days festival and enjoy the peak bloom. The celebration includes a flower show, wine tasting, square dancing, and a host of activities contributing to the merriment.

❀ **Admission:** Free.

Garden open: 8:00 A.M. to 7:00 P.M. on festival days (in general, the second half of May).

Further information: Call or check Web site for open dates, bloom status, and directions. Up-to-date festival details are posted on the Web site. Display gardens are wheelchair accessible.

Directions: Cooley's is located just outside Silverton, 9 miles east of Salem. Take Silverton Road from Salem directly to Cooley's. Detailed driving directions from Portland and a map are found on the Web site.

8. The Oregon Garden

879 West Main Street, **Silverton**, OR 97381 (mailing address: The Oregon Garden Foundation, P.O. Box 155, Silverton, OR 97381); (503) 874–8100, (877) 674–2733; www.oregongarden.org

A GROUNDBREAKING celebration in June 1997 heralded the official opening of the Oregon Garden, an eighty-acre setting conceived by the Oregon Association of Nurseries to showcase the choicest plants grown and propagated in the Pacific Northwest region. You'll discover an ambitious undertaking: a garden that celebrates the aesthetic pleasures and educational aspects of horticulture and botany.

The 2004 season introduced a new visitor center on the garden's upper level, providing entree to the garden and wonderful views as well. Graced by skylights and large sections of glass walls, the building houses a gift shop, cafe, and a centralized place where visitors can gather information. You'll see the Natural Resources Education Center nearby and the admission kiosk on the adjacent Overlook plaza, the garden's main walkway.

The A-Mazing Water Garden emerges not far from the entrance area, taking in one acre devoted to ornamental water plants, carnivorous species, and tropical cultivars. An adjacent wetlands complex utilizes treated water that pours forth into ponds and pools, creating a habitat for flora as well as wildlife.

Currently, there are more than twenty specially designed theme gardens in both formal layouts and naturalistic areas.

On the plaza the design of the Bosque calls attention to dozens of container-grown Pacific Sunset maples. The design features still pools of water surrounding squares of brickwork that outline the soil at the base of each tree. The overall composition results in planted trees that appear to float on the water's surface.

Not far from the visitor center and a stairway to the pavilion, a Sensory Garden offers its myriad pleasures to all, but especially to visitors with physical challenges. A decorative cedar trellis, upright wall gardens, and a rain curtain come together to create an enfolding milieu brimming with scented flora and tactile characteristics.

Look for the Rose Petal Fountain, where you can observe a wealth of brilliant annuals in a setting bolstered by an enthralling vista of the Willamette Valley.

The Children's Garden provides space for hands-on experiences aimed at delighting children, including plants geared toward arousing the interest of youngsters. Special children's programming often takes place informally on weekends or during special events such as Earth Day.

Hundreds of trees were planted at the garden's outset to beautify the surroundings. Yet the landscape encompasses the admirable prospect of a twenty-five-acre grove of native oaks. You'll come upon the stature of one of Oregon's landmark Heritage Trees—the venerable Signature Oak Tree, hundreds of years old.

Well worth seeking out is the peerless collection of dwarf conifers in the Conifer Garden. The Western Chapter of the American Conifer Society was instrumental in developing this world-class alliance of eye-catching specimens that reveal myriad shapes, foliage textures, and tantalizing hues. To harmonize with and counterbalance the evergreen species, the garden also embraces heaths and heathers, fragrant daphnes, Japanese maples, and the like.

On a high point, at the top of Oregon Way, the Axis Fountain looms. Constructed of Montana stone, the fountain's form is complemented by a section of tumbling water. Multilevel seating and valley views entice one to stop and spend time enjoying the refreshing scene.

In 2001 the only house in Oregon to be designed by acclaimed architect Frank Lloyd Wright was relocated to a site on the grounds of the Oregon Garden. The restored Gordon House is now situated in an oak grove, a short distance from the garden entrance. With its stunning floor-to-ceiling windows and cantilevered profile, the Gordon House is yours to discover on a self-guided tour of the main floor, a guided tour of the house, or on a group tour.

There's much more to see. Once a Christmas tree plantation, the Rediscovery Forest presents an instructive exhibit on how trees grow and forests evolve. In the Northwest Garden, local gardeners and visitors alike find design ideas and inspiration in the plants that are highlighted. Near the business office, the Pet Friendly Garden offers pet owners an instructive look at the best specimens to consider planting and others to avoid. East of the Signature Oak tree, look for the Lewis and Clark Plant Collection Garden, bringing botanical history to life.

✿ **Admission:** Fee.

Garden open: Daily 10:00 A.M. to 6:00 P.M. from May through September; daily 10:00 A.M. to 4:00 P.M. from October through April. Call before visiting to confirm hours. Gordon House is open daily 10:00 A.M. to 5:00 P.M. May through September and 10:00 A.M. to 4:00 P.M. October through April. The last guided house tour begins one hour before closing.

Further information: The gift shop carries gardening books and assorted paraphernalia. Call for information on tram tours. Check the Web site for an up-to-date listing of news and events. Call the Gordon House museum office at (503) 874–6006 to learn about afternoon teas or special cultural activities. Most of the garden is wheelchair accessible.

Directions: The Oregon Garden is 42 miles south of Portland, about fifteen minutes west of I–5, To reach the garden from downtown Salem, take Silverton Road (Highway 213) 15 miles east to the southern outskirts of historic Silverton, bordering the Cascade foothills. Call or look on the Web site for detailed directions from points north or south.

South Willamette Valley and Southern Oregon Gardenwalks

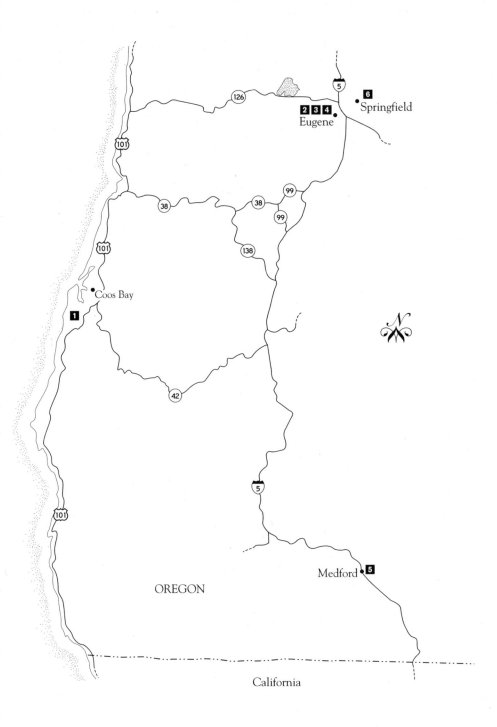

126

5

2 3 4
Eugene

6
• Springfield

101

38

38

99

99

138

101

• Coos Bay

1

42

N

5

OREGON

Medford • 5

California

1. Coos Bay: Shore Acres
   State Park Garden
2. Eugene: Greer Gardens
3. Eugene: Hendricks Park
   Rhododendron Garden
4. Eugene: Owen Memorial
   Rose Garden
5. Medford: Siskiyou
   Rare Plant Nursery
6. Springfield: Gossler Farms
   Nursery

1. Shore Acres State Park Garden

89039 Cape Arago Highway, **Coos Bay,** OR 97420 (mailing address: Sunset Bay Management Unit, 89814 Cape Arago Highway, Coos Bay, OR 97420); (541) 888–3732, (866) 888-6100 (gift center); www.shoreacres.net, www.oregonstateparks.org

$\mathcal{V}$ ISITORS encounter a dramatic coastal setting at Shore Acres State Park, originally the baronial summer estate of Louis Simpson, who made his fortune in shipbuilding and the timber trade. The state of Oregon assumed control of the property in 1942, and in 1986 the Friends of Shore Acres, Inc., was formed to provide educational, interpretive, and physical development programs for the Sunset Bay Management Unit, which includes Shore Acres and other state parks.

Although Simpson's mansion is long gone, the historic landscape poised high above the Pacific Ocean boasts seven acres of beautifully restored gardens encircled by spruce, cypress, and pine trees. Flowering shrubs and perennials produce a parade of color.

When you enter Shore Acres, the lovely English rose garden unfolds before you, with its patterned outline defined by crisply clipped hedges. Meander through the roses, veering to the right, and you come upon another eye-catching feature: an expansive pergola.

The property's stately past is discernible as you proceed beyond the rose garden's hedging, linked directly to the structural enclosure of a formal garden. Going forward, you'll enjoy a serene vision, where the distinguished hardscaping creates an overall framework for emerald lawns wrapping around radiant beds and borders. Next to the formal garden is the Garden House; sometimes referred to as the "gardener's cottage," it is the only remaining structure from Simpson's era.

Along the perimeter area, the Observation Building has sprung up where the Simpson house once stood. Its site by the breathtaking cliffs affords unforgettable vistas throughout the year.

There is more to experience here, from a Japanese pond garden to an All-America Rose Selections display garden. Presiding over the gardens is a towering example of *Pinus radiata*, honored by being included on a national registry of significant trees. This majestic Monterey pine dates from 1910 or so, when it beautified the Simpson estate.

If you favor spring bulbs, plan to visit from the end of February through April, when daffodil displays merge with tulips. A riot of "rhodies" and azaleas follows into the month of May. Seasonal shows continue with bevies of annuals and perennials into the fall. The summer months are fragrant with roses; a collection of dahlias is especially gratifying from August into the middle of October.

The Shore Acres gardens demonstrate their own particular magic from Thanksgiving through the New Year with an enchanting exhibition of 250,000 colored holiday lights and decorations in the gardens. In the late afternoons and the evenings, generally from 4:00 to 10:00, visitors can revel in the heavenly backdrop while enjoying cookies and hot drinks.

Don't miss the cliff walk, where the ocean's pounding surf provides a thrilling prospect. Here, too, you can view the winter and spring whale migration. The trail leading to Simpson Beach and a secreted, out-of-the-way cove presents an extremely intriguing foray.

Enhanced by charming formal gardens, Shore Acres State Park can proudly claim an inviting atmosphere crowned by fine horticulture. It's a testament to the dedication of park staff and the partnership between the Oregon Parks and Recreation Department and the Friends group.

Admission: Free; parking fee charged for vehicles.

Garden open: Daily 8:00 A.M. to sunset. Call to confirm the 10:00 P.M. closing during the Holiday Lights and Open House.

Further information: The gift center is open for seasonal hours; call or check the Shore Acres Web site. Look on the Web site for a calendar of special events, more details on the holiday celebrations, and a map of the gardens. The information and gift center is situated next to the garden's handsome new entrance. The garden is wheelchair accessible.

Directions: Shore Acres is 13 miles off U.S. Highway 101; from the towns of Coos Bay and North Bend follow the signs to the state parks. A detailed map can be found at www.shoreacres.net.

2. Greer Gardens

1280 Goodpasture Island Road, **Eugene,** OR 97401; (541) 686–8266, (800) 548–0111; www.greergardens.com

APRIL and May give rise to heavenly visions at Greer Gardens, where stunning collections of azaleas and rhododendrons can be expected to peak around Mother's Day. At this fine nursery you can procure unusual perennials, maples, bonsai, mature trees, and shrubs of many kinds. These plants endow the premises with radiant foliage, flowers, and intriguing bark textures throughout the year. You'll also find plants displaying a range of branching habits, from upright, pyramidal, and weeping forms to prostrate, creeping types fit for any sort of landscape plan.

Business is chiefly by mail order at this Eugene, Oregon, establishment, but the Greer Gardens' sales area and display gardens are open to the public year-round. When you visit, be sure to tour the nursery's growing fields and investigate the book department's laudable selection of gardening books.

Widely appealing to plant lovers, the extensive Greer Gardens' inventory also includes blue Himalayan poppies, rare clematis species and cultivars, uncommon deciduous azaleas, ornamental grasses, and bamboo.

❀ **Admission:** Free.

Garden open: Monday through Saturday 8:30 A.M. to 5:30 P.M., Sunday 11:00 A.M. to 5 P.M.

Further information: Paths are hilly; golf carts are available. Wheelchair access is limited.

Directions: Greer Gardens is a ten-minute drive north of downtown Eugene. Take Interstate 5 to exit 195B and travel west on Beltline Highway to the Delta Highway exit. On Delta Highway, take the Goodpasture Island Road exit and go east ⅓ mile to the nursery. Call before visiting to confirm directions, or look on the Web site for a map.

3. Hendricks Park Rhododendron Garden

1800 Skyline Boulevard at Summit Avenue, **Eugene,** OR 97403;
(541) 682–5324, (541) 682–4800 (main parks office);
www.ci.eugene.or.us

*I*N A PARK encompassing some eighty acres, you'll find a shimmering twelve-acre Pacific Northwest setting devoted to more than 6,000 rhododendrons in combination with ornamental plantings of bulbs, perennials, and fine woody specimens like viburnums and witch hazels.

The Main Garden Walk ribbons around a one-acre swath of emerald turf in a setting where Oregon white oaks hold sway. Myriad flowering shrubs and trees begin to bloom in January, with the spectacle stretching well into July.

Picnic Places

You can turn your gardenwalk at the Hendricks Park Rhododendron Garden in Eugene into a daylong adventure. Picnic tables are arranged in the gardens, making it a fine place to bring a lunch and spend a relaxing afternoon. The riverfront setting is linked to a bike path, ideal for anyone inclined to mix garden exploration with cycling.

Count upon mid-April to signal the apex of the rhodies, together with the glorious blossoms of *Magnolia* 'Picture', bursting forth in a springtime feast for the senses.

At Hendricks, the vast groupings of rhododendrons are featured in numbered planting beds. Arranged according to harmonious color themes, Beds 3, 4 and 6, for instance, are an early-season highlight, taking in species and varieties set out in a pleasing blend of creamy hues playing off pink flowers. The season progresses with the hugely showy, heavenly scented blooms of *Rhododendron* 'Loderi King George.' At the same time, deciduous azaleas vie for attention with their spectacular color contrasts from violet to orange to crimson.

Look for the James Barto Walk to loop around, going up toward the Main Garden Walk. Bed 22 appears where the Barto Walk begins, and a vivid flounce of purple heralds February as the species *R. ririei* blooms. Other lovely species exhibit blue, purple, and pink flowers at the top of this walk in May.

Seek out the Del James Walk, adjoining the southwest section of the Main Garden Walk. Terraces adorn the sloped terrain here, showcasing a fascinating collection of plants that once embellished the James home.

Located above the Rhododendron Garden (to the east), a native plant garden emerges next to the F. M. Wilkins picnic shelter.

Fawn lilies, irises, and trilliums are a few of the magical natives appearing seasonally in this new area under development.

Situated on a high point overlooking the cities of Eugene and Springfield, the Hendricks Park Rhododendron Garden is equipped with plenty of benches for a welcome respite from your travels. You are welcome to breathe in the greenery and gaze out upon the compelling vistas.

❀ **Admission:** Free.

Garden open: Daylight hours until 11:00 P.M.

Further information: A calendar of events for the rhododendron garden, as well as additional details for both it and the native plant garden, can be found on the Web site. The rhododendron garden is limited in terms of wheelchair access due to its hilly trails: There is a main loop that is accessible. Excellent views of Eugene and the rhododendrons can be enjoyed from various parking areas, too.

Directions: Follow Franklin Boulevard (Highway 99), and turn south onto Walnut Street. Turn south again onto Fairmount Boulevard, and turn east onto Summit Avenue, proceeding up the hill to where Summit Avenue, Floral Hill Drive, and Birch Lane intersect. Parking lots are located to the right and to the left.

4. Owen Memorial Rose Garden

North end of Jefferson Street off First Avenue, **Eugene,** OR
(mailing address: 1820 Roosevelt Boulevard, Eugene, OR 97402);
(541) 682–4800; www.ci.eugene.or.us

*L*ANE COUNTY, Oregon, offers many delightful garden forays, among them the nine-acre Owen Memorial Rose Garden boasting 4,500 roses. Savor fragrant collections of species roses, miniatures, polyanthas, and climbing types: In all, some 400 varieties of roses await visitors.

An All-America Rose Selections display garden encompasses exciting new varieties, with additional arrays of modern roses that include hybrid tea, floribunda, and grandiflora types.

The design of the garden borders and beds mingles formal areas with more casual plantings, set off by an attractive pergola and arbor. Perennials and bulbs, magnolias and silk trees enhance the landscape as the seasons turn. A recent feature appears on the west side of the Owen House, where beds of Japanese iris grow, a donation from Eugene's sister city in Kakegawa, Japan.

At the beginning of April, visitors who proceed to the north end of the garden behold the state's largest cherry tree. Dating from 1860, the Black Republican Cherry is a grand sight anytime, but especially when wearing its spectacular springtime cloak of frothy white blossoms. The lone survivor of a long-ago orchard, the tree reigns over the scenery; its heavy branches now require posts for support.

Early to mid-June is generally when the peak rose bloom occurs, but bright flowers are on exhibit throughout the summer and into the early part of fall.

❀ **Admission:** Free.

Garden open: Daylight to 11:00 P.M.

Further information: Visit the city's Web site for details on the garden's history. Paths are mostly wheelchair accessible. You'll find plenty of parking available.

Directions: Owen Memorial Rose Garden is centrally located in the city of Eugene, along the south bank of the Willamette River. Follow Jefferson Street, a main thoroughfare, north toward the river. The rose gardens emerge at the end of the street.

5. Siskiyou Rare Plant Nursery

2825 Cummings Road, **Medford,** OR 97501; (541) 772–6846;
www.siskiyourareplantnursery.com

*S*ISKIYOU boasts a track record of forty years or so devoted to growing rare plants. The nursery owner and manager for the past twenty-five years, Baldassare Mineo conveys to his nursery's dedicated clientele both an unbridled enthusiasm and a discerning eye for unusual garden selections.

Siskiyou's two-acre garden highlights the nursery's specialty—exceptional alpine plants. At the same time Mineo applies his artistic background to creating pleasing arrangements of plant material. Countless dwarf and miniature plants thrive in refined rock garden settings. You'll also find a verdant landscape of distinctive perennials, ornamental grasses, miniature conifers, Japanese maples, hardy ferns, and uncommon shrubs and trees.

Since many new plant introductions are growing in the display gardens, visitors can see a specimen's horticultural attributes firsthand, getting inspiration and ideas to help in selecting plants or in creating their own alluring combinations. Now extremely popular, the drought-tolerant variety *Gaura lindheimeri* 'Siskiyou Pink', for instance, was introduced some years ago by the nursery. Today it's a favorite of gardeners everywhere.

Mid-April through May is generally the peak blooming period at Siskiyou Rare Plant Nursery, which is located in southwest Oregon's Rogue Valley. Still, you can count upon the area's beneficial climate for an animated exhibition of plants throughout the open season.

Like a magnet, the nursery's sale area draws savvy gardeners to peruse thousands of available plants, looking for particularly choice varieties to fill out the garden plan at home.

🏵 **Admission:** Free.

Garden open: Tuesday through Friday 9:00 A.M. to 5:00 P.M. and the first Saturday of each month 9:00 A.M. to 2:00 P.M. from March through October; closed the first Saturday in July. (*Note:* Baldassare says to guarantee that you get all the plants you want from the catalog or Web site, send your order in two weeks in advance and your order will be ready for pick up when you arrive for a visit.) If visiting off-season, from November through February, arrange appointments two weeks in advance.

Further information: Call or click on Contact Us on the Web site to make appointment or for tour information. Wheelchair access is limited. **Directions:** The nursery's Medford location is 30 miles north of the California border after driving through the Siskiyou Mountains, or a five-hour drive from Portland. Take I–5 to exit 33 (Central Point) and travel east on Biddle Road; turn south onto Table Rock Road, then turn east onto Midway Road, and take a left onto Cummings Road. Look on the Web site for a map showing the nursery's location.

6. Gossler Farms Nursery

1200 Weaver Road, **Springfield,** OR 97478; (541) 746–3922; www.gosslerfarms.com

ONE OF THE foremost nurseries located in the Pacific Northwest, Gossler Farms Nursery is a family-run enterprise operated by Eric, Roger, and Marj Gossler. The property's alluvial soil provides excellent growing conditions for a breathtaking collection of plants. When you tour the nursery's extensive display gardens, you'll see a flourishing palette of plant material.

Among the nursery's specialties are foliage plants with beautiful fall color, fragrant viburnums, and dogwood varieties. The nursery has gained a reputation for splendid magnolias, too, and spring is perhaps the optimum time to observe in the neighborhood of 500 glorious selections growing in the nursery's garden. Some one hundred types are offered for sale.

Savvy gardeners call on the Gosslers when seeking an introduction to the eccentric characteristics and enticing design possibilities of witch hazels. *Hamamelis* species and uncommon cultivars are abundantly represented in the repertoire of 5,000 select plant varieties on view at the nursery.

Wend your way through the garden's mixed borders and take in the painterly combinations of perennials, bulbs, trees, and shrubs. Garden travelers will find the verdant flora and unusual blooms brightening the scenery year-round.

Schedule an appointment when you want to purchase praiseworthy specimens for your home garden. You'll find fascinating plant associations, replanted and freshened each year to provide maximum interest. You can also place an order to have selections shipped. With wonderful plants suitable for gardens found throughout the U.S. Department of Agriculture's hardiness zones, Gossler Farms Nursery is deserving of its acclaim.

❀ **Admission:** Free.

Garden open: Appointment by phone required. Also open the first weekend of each month: Friday, Saturday, and Sunday 9:00 A.M. to 4:00 P.M., excluding holiday weekends.

Further information: Call in advance to arrange a visit and to confirm open hours. Look for news of special events on the Web site. Walkways are paved and accessible to wheelchairs.

Directions: Gossler Farms Nursery is located east of Eugene, 9 miles from I–5. Call for directions or look for a detailed map on the Web site.

Garden Lodgings

*L*IKE MANY travelers who maintain full, even jam-packed itineraries, I sometimes yearn for a quiet place to unwind at the end of a heavily scheduled day of trekking from one garden destination to another. It's not the confines of a rented room I seek, but rather a secluded, preferably verdant area for contemplation.

The congenial bed-and-breakfast inns recommended here provide guests with the customary amenities, and then some. In general, you'll find luscious breakfasts and freshly baked snacks, complimentary beverages, private baths, and furnishings intended for your comfort and pleasure.

Criteria for inclusion, however, extend beyond such desirable attributes. In the end it was a special sort of aesthetic sensibility, perhaps best described as a naturalistic style of garden design, which I found to be the most inviting.

In my attempts to find places that would add an element of enchantment to each day's sojourn, I looked for agreeable proprietors who maintain relaxed settings. Sites range from convivial family-run establishments to properties offering fine dining and expansive grounds.

Whether you like a quiet stroll before breakfast or require a few minutes to breathe in the night air after an evening meal, serene and private places await.

Please note that cancellation policies vary. Always request details when phoning for reservations.

✿ Price Code

The following price code is for two adults. The codes do not include taxes and other fees. Prices are in U.S. dollars.

$	$60 to $145
$$	$146 to $260
$$$	$261 to $399
$$$$	More than $400

BRITISH COLUMBIA

Sooke Harbour House

> 1528 Whiffen Spit Road, **Sooke**, BC V0S 1N0 (Vancouver Island); (250) 642-3421, (800) 889-9688; www.sookeharbourhouse.com

SOOKE HARBOUR HOUSE completed a thirteen-room expansion a while ago, and at that time the inn's premier culinary garden was reorganized and replanted. Both the inn's gardens and the bountiful sea yield important ingredients for the regional Northwest Coast cuisine of Sooke Harbour House's restaurant, which draws diners from around the world. Having garnered countless accolades, the restaurant and its imaginative gourmet fare are legendary.

In the gardens wild native plants figure prominently among hundreds of edible items that are cultivated alongside leeks and kales, lavender and rosemary. Foods that once offered sustenance to the region's First Nation's people—nodding onion, wild thimble,

The Whiffen Spit and Sooke Harbour House

Vibrant works of art are on view throughout Sooke Harbour House and its grounds, from each guest room to the interior of an elevator (in the guise of an undersea adventure), the gallery-style hallway filled with paintings, and the inner niche set off by sculpture. Equally artful gardens are on tour each morning at 10:30. The tours are open to guests and the public alike. Especially noteworthy is the environmentally wise "green" parking lot that combines grass turf and a recycled plastic grid set in sand.

The unique location of this country inn offers another unparalleled prospect: the Whiffen Spit. Personally, I'm fascinated by earthworks and the feelings these creations give rise to—works such as Robert Smithson's *Spiral Jetty* or Alain Idoux's *Lavender Wedge*, the latter an example of French land art. During a visit to Sooke, you'll "discover" a sandy spit of land that nature created, and perhaps, like me, you will fall under its spell. Wake early on a misty morning and walk out to explore the spit, your footsteps tracing the landform's ¾-mile curvilinear pattern sketched into sheltered Sooke Harbour. Take in a bit of top-notch birdwatching or stroll along the spit with the sun overhead, feasting all the while on a vista of the Olympic Mountains that emerges as a backdrop to complete the serene scene.

and salal berries; the young light green needles of grand firs; and licorice fern root—contribute to the highly original cuisine enjoyed by the restaurant's patrons.

Menus emphasize the freshest ingredients found locally in season. Seafood and shellfish are especially popular. Dishes may feature sea urchin, gooseneck barnacles, or geoduck. Edible seaweed or a squid ink sauce might appear in an entree together with a cornucopia of freshly harvested edible flowers. At Sooke Harbour House, tuberous begonias and Johnny-jump-ups are colorful companions in mélanges featuring chickweeds, lamb's-quarters and wild sorrel for more savory salad flavors.

Set on a bluff overlooking the Olympic Peninsula and Juan de Fuca Strait, Sooke Harbour House offers spectacular views. When visiting the inn, you may wish to accompany a gardener on a mid-morning tour to study the attractively planted gardens. Each gardener has specific knowledge and expertise: medicinal plant properties, for instance, or culinary uses of plants, or decorative design of herb gardens. Getting a close look at what is surely one of the most fruitful culinary gardens associated with a bed-and-breakfast retreat should not be missed.

Be sure to check the Web site to view a calendar of events. You will find news of all sorts of delightful possibilities, from a festival celebrating wine to a creative writing workshop and weekend adventures dedicated to cuisine.

✿ **Rates:** $$–$$$$.

Open: Year-round. Look on the Web site or call for details and dates on partial winter closures.

Facilities: Sooke Harbour Houses is a full service country inn featuring twenty-eight rooms, a spa, a gallery, and the restaurant. Room rates include breakfast; a picnic lunch is also included seasonally. Two rooms are wheelchair accessible.

Directions: The inn is located 23 miles west of Victoria, about 1 mile from the village of Sooke. Driving from Victoria, take Trans-Canada Highway 1 north to the Sooke turnoff at exit 14, Veteran's Memorial Parkway. Follow Veteran's Memorial Parkway, turning right onto Highway 14 west, and continue to the village of Sooke; then turn left onto Whiffen Spit Road. A map and detailed directions are found on the Web site.

Abigail's Hotel

906 McClure Street, **Victoria,** BC V8V 3E7 (Vancouver Island);
(250) 388–5363, (800) 561–6565; www.abigailshotel.com

A GLIMPSE of Abigail's striking Tudor facade hints at the comfort and ambience this jewel of a hotel promises guests. Conveniently located just a few blocks from downtown Victoria and the city's Inner Harbour, the renovated and redecorated Abigail's offers an intimate atmosphere on a par with what one finds in any top European-style hotel.

Canopy and four-poster beds, plush goosedown comforters, refreshing Jacuzzis, and luscious breakfasts all make you feel that you've landed in the lap of luxury. Abigail's is the perfect place to regroup before embarking on another day of garden outings. In the evening you can nibble on hors d'oeuvres and enjoy a sherry in the library. Around the handsome stone fireplace, you can chat with Abigail's gracious staff and find out more about this registered historic building.

Keep in mind the city of Victoria's reputation for glorious floral displays. The small heritage gardens in front of the hotel buildings afford guests the added pleasure of identifying perennial favorites while guessing the names of less-familiar plants on a walk around the grounds.

Two blocks south of Abigail's Hotel, explore Beacon Hill Park (see the gardenwalk entry), where naturalized daffodils lend a lustrous glow to a February stroll. One of countless verdant oases in the province of British Columbia, the 120-acre park includes blooming borders and a glistening pond. Ocean walkways, overlooking the Strait of Juan de Fuca, provide spectacular vistas of the distant Olympic Peninsula, good weather prevailing.

✿ **Rates:** $–$$$.
Open: Year-round.
Facilities: Twenty-three rooms with private baths; gourmet breakfasts

served. The coach house's six rooms and three honeymoon suites all feature a queen or king bed, double Jacuzzi, and wood-burning fireplace. Parking is free for guests; the hotel is entirely nonsmoking.

Directions: Abigail's is on McClure Street, 1 block south of Burdett Avenue and a few blocks east of the Inner Harbour (directly east of Quadra Street). Detailed directions are found on the Web site; to see a map, click on Getting Here.

Markham House Bed & Breakfast

1853 Connie Road, **Victoria,** BC V9C 4C2 (Vancouver Island); (250) 642–7542, (888) 256–6888; www.markhamhouse.com

TUDOR-STYLE Markham House is situated on a ten-acre estate of sloping lawns and landscaped gardens in a hillside setting graced by mature conifers and a lush tapestry of vegetation. Anyone with a passion for flowers will swoon over Markham House's approximately one hundred varieties of tall bearded iris. Blooming from around mid-May through the middle of June, the irises create a transcendent expanse of color bordering the lower lawns. You'll behold the sumptuous ruffled pink of 'Beverly Sills' and the extraordinarily beautiful 'Rolling Thunder', of deepest purple. A favorite of Lyall Markham's, 'Peach Picotee', is distinguished by its salmon-colored fall (the flower's downward-hanging outer petals) and pinkish standard (its three more erect inner petals).

Garden areas are both formal and informal. With its woodland backdrop, the trout pond on the house's north side exhibits a wild beauty. Richly planted with spring-blooming rhododendrons, the pond is surrounded by rushes and gunnera (commonly called "dinosaur food" for its gargantuan leaves). Siberian irises, with their flowers in hues of burgundy and white, add stunning accents to this setting, where nature's random exuberance meets the gardener's guiding hand.

Accommodations are located in the inn's guest wing. Three bedrooms with country charm look out over the picture-perfect scenery. Each bedroom includes a fireplace and private bathroom. The Garden Suite features a double spa tub set in a window overlooking the pond. All guests are invited to partake of the full-size hot tub in the gazebo on the edge of the forest.

Inhabiting its own secluded nook, Honeysuckle Cottage is found up the garden path. The cottage's woodstove and lovely slate hearth add warmth and beauty to a cozy renovated interior. The cottage is complete with a bedroom, a living area, a bathroom, a private hot tub on the deck, and an antique pine wardrobe that hides a small yet serviceable kitchen.

In balmy weather the Markhams serve tea on the patio, where you have a fine view of the genteel landscape with its picturesque trout pond. During winter months a crackling fire indoors establishes an inviting tea time atmosphere.

❄ **Rates:** $–$$. (Call to check on availability of discounts.)
Open: Year-round.
Facilities: Four rooms; all with private baths. Full gourmet breakfast is served.
Directions: Markham House is approximately thirty-five minutes west of the capital city of Victoria, 10 minutes east of the village of Sooke. Take Trans-Canada 1 north to the Sooke/Port Renfrew exit, where you will go over the highway, and turn onto Highway 14 south. Turn onto Highway 14 west and drive about fifteen minutes to the Markham House sign. Turn left onto Connie Road. You'll find a detailed map and directions on the Web site.

WASHINGTON

Bainbridge Island Lodging Association

www.bainbridgelodging.com

ALL TOGETHER, the three dozen or so members affiliated with the Bainbridge Island Lodging Association suggest a treasure trove of places to stay. And the wide range of rates should fit most any budget.

You'll discover traditional bed-and-breakfast accommodations located in inviting homes and chance upon sequestered cottages in countryside settings, complete with amenities such as fully equipped kitchens, hot tubs, and fireplaces.

There are lodgings with arresting views of Puget Sound and Seattle and waterfront sites tailor-made for those who love beach-combing and the sound of waves lapping at the shore. Accommodations highlighting privacy may appeal to visitors looking for a romantic hideaway. The types of lodgings cover a wide scope.

Waterfall Gardens Private Suites, for one, is a bucolic five-acre retreat enlivened by spring-fed ponds and a restored salmon creek. A property that had once been overrun with brambles is now planted with hundreds of native trees, some reaching 60 feet tall, together with arrays of natives such as sword ferns and evergreen huckleberries.

Strolling amid the totally organic, naturalistic gardens in this "eco-friendly sanctuary" is a special treat, as the riparian habitat running along the salmon steam attracts abundant wildlife. Nature lovers will be drawn to observe herons and kingfishers, among dozens of bird species that have been sighted here.

At Fuurin-Oka Futon & Breakfast, you'll happen upon a refreshingly unique setting. Here visitors encounter a traditional Japanese house and garden designed and built by the innkeeper, a gifted architect. The co-innkeeper counts gardening acumen among her many talents.

A gathering of flowering shrubs and pretty foliage plants graces the parking area: camellia, viburnum, nandina, and Japanese maple, to name a few. Follow the flagstone pathway through the wooden gate as you approach the house's entrance, and you'll experience the verdant atmosphere of a bamboo grove.

In this setting, the east and west boundaries are enhanced by eight bamboo varieties commingling with fragrant sarcoccoca and

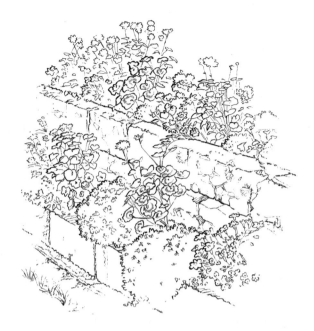

Kerria japonica. Alongside the veranda a courtyard garden unfolds, abetted by Hinoki falsecypress and a mature Japanese maple grown from a cutting. The maple's record of ancestry is fascinating, reaching back to a tree grown in Tokyo's Imperial Palace garden and to its scion, which grew in the Washington Park Arboretum's Japanese Garden until its demise due to a fire.

Iris, Scotch moss, and shaped box make up an alliance adorning the inn's graceful water feature. Here a tableau of a small stream, waterfall, and pond is counterbalanced by a weeping blue Atlantic cedar. The sculptural form of a contorted hazel accentuates the crest of a hill, while eye-catching displays highlight areas of the grounds throughout the seasons, from tree peony and Korean lilac to heavenly scented rhododendrons and azaleas.

The lodgings span a geographic area that crisscrosses Bainbridge Island and extends to the Kitsap Peninsula and Poulsbo area. A stay at any member's accommodation should find you well situated to visit numerous gardens around the region. Whether one's preference is for contemporary architecture and modern decor or Craftsman style, a stately manor filled with antiques or an out-of the-ordinary retreat, it's likely you will find a suitably pleasing lodging.

Look on the Web site for the lodging map to see the locations of listed members. Click on any member icon for further details on rates, facilities, and directions as well as links to many distinctive Web sites hosted by individual members.

Chambered Nautilus Bed & Breakfast Inn

5005 Twenty-second Avenue NE, **Seattle,** WA 98105;
(206) 522–2536, (800) 545–8459; www.chamberednautilus.com

HOUSED IN a pretty 1915 Georgian colonial, the Chambered Nautilus is conveniently situated in the city's university district. The inn sits perched on a high knoll, affording views of the Cascade Mountains. Located close to downtown for easy access to Pike Place Market (a visit there is an obligatory, pleasantly diverting activity on any visit to Seattle), and within walking distance from the University of Washington, the inn has a gracious vintage ambience—comfortably cozy, yet delightfully unfussy.

Decor at the Chambered Nautilus is just as the inn's brochure states—that is, "classic Seattle style." Antiques blend agreeably with refined pieces to achieve a relaxed look. Expect a warm welcome from the innkeepers, who exemplify the amiable disposition associated with this appealing city.

Seasonal displays of bulbs punctuate the flower beds wrapping around the inn. Early in the year, fragrant daphne blooms by the front door, while rosemary, thyme, and other herbs consort with euphorbias, colorful maples, showy hydrangeas, and vibrant red poppies. A welcoming swath of lawn at the back of the inn overlooks a shade garden where visitors can take a relaxing time-out. Just across the lawn, a four-unit building nestles into a wooded area enhanced by lots of greenery. The inn's newest suites are located here, offering nightly visits or extended stays.

Successfully combining a casual mood with just the right degree of pampering and personal attention, the Chambered Nautilus promises a perfect home base for your garden travels. In close proximity you'll find the University of Washington's Medicinal Herb Garden (see the gardenwalk entry). The Washington Park Arboretum and Japanese Garden are within easy reach, either by car or public transportation.

❁ **Rates:** $–$$.

Open: Year-round.

Facilities: Six nonsmoking rooms with private baths. Enjoy the botanical motif of the Garden Chamber room, with king bed, large porch with views, and detached private bath. The romantic Rose Chamber room boasts a porch overlooking the gardens, while the spacious Scallop Chamber offers a queen bed, private rear porch, gas fireplace, and dormer window with vistas of the Cascades. Bathrobes, bottled water, private phones with voice mail, wireless Internet access, and well-stocked bookshelves are a few of the amenities provided. In all, four rooms feature porches affording views of the garden or Cascade Mountains. A business center in the living room allows you to print your own boarding passes before leaving for the airport. Delicious gourmet breakfasts are served. The suites adjacent to the inn feature private entrances, kitchenettes, and more.

Directions: Chambered Nautilus is located next to the University of Washington campus in Seattle's University District. From Interstate 5 take the Fiftieth Street exit. Travel east on Fiftieth until it nearly ends at Twentieth Avenue NE. Look for the flashing red stoplight at this intersection, then turn left onto Twentieth Avenue NE, continuing to Fifty-fourth Street. Turn right onto Fifty-fourth Street. At the bottom of the hill, turn right on Twenty-second Avenue NE. A detailed map and directions are found on the Web site.

Chelsea Station on the Park

4915 Linden Avenue North, **Seattle,** WA 98103; (206) 547–6077,
(800) 400–6077; www.bandbseattle.com

CHELSEA STATION on the Park bed-and-breakfast consists of lodgings located in two handsome redbrick, federal colonial–style buildings. The inn's welcoming atmosphere results in part from the
uncluttered beauty of its mission-style furnishings.

At Chelsea Station you'll enjoy a high level of comfort, terrific
breakfasts, and gracious innkeepers who dispense the type of cordial,
helpful counsel traditionally associated with bed-and-breakfast inns
but not necessarily the norm these days. Whether you require directions for your garden visits, dining advice, or help in getting around
town on buses, the innkeepers will point you in the right direction.

Chelsea Station is adjacent to the lovely Woodland Park Rose
Garden, within easy distance by car or public transportation to the
Medicinal Herb Garden at the University of Washington, and not
far from Washington Park's fine Arboretum and Japanese Garden
(see the Seattle and East King County chapter).

Just across Fiftieth Street, enter Woodland Park for easy access
to the extensive natural habitat of Woodland Park Zoo. Minutes
away, the Fremont neighborhood is an artistic mecca filled with
bookstores, galleries, colorful shops, restaurants, and inviting cafes
all wonderful for people watching.

❀ **Rates:** $–$$.

Open: Year-round.

Facilities: Nine rooms and suites with private baths; views of the Cascade Mountains enhance some of the rooms. The spacious Margaret
Suite features a king bed, sitting area, and lovely views of Seattle and
Mount Rainier. The Woodland Park Suite offers its own private
entrance and phone line, while another smaller suite overlooks the rose
garden across the street. Economy-minded travelers may wish to book
the Iris or Greenlake Rooms in the inn's quiet rear area. Each features

a queen bed and in-room phone. A full breakfast is served; freshly baked cookies and hot beverages are available throughout the day.

Directions: The inn is centrally located in Seattle's North End, on Linden Avenue between Highway 99 and Fremont Avenue North, off North Fiftieth Street. A detailed map, transportation information, and driving directions can be found on the Web site.

OREGON

Youngberg Hill Vineyards & Inn

10660 Southwest Youngberg Hill Road, **McMinnville,** OR 97128; (503) 472–2727, (888) 657–8668; www.youngberghill.com

ON A TWELVE-ACRE vineyard in Oregon wine country, Youngberg Hill Vineyards Inn is surrounded by rolling hills and refreshing views of the Willamette Valley, the Cascades, and the Coast Range. The lovely grounds combine the atmosphere of a natural setting with plantings of perennials and annuals.

The inn's farmhouse perches picturesquely atop a hill on the vineyard estate, which encompasses 50 acres. Around the estate are more than 800 acres of farmed and forested land. The bed-and-breakfast Craftsman-style inn promises a convenient resting place for day trips to the area's many exceptional plant nurseries or a foray to the Oregon Garden (see the gardenwalk entry).

Guests are encouraged to stroll through the vineyards. You'll also come upon a newly landscaped spot set off by a gazebo. A concert series is one of the special happenings taking place here: when planning your visit, you can access a calendar of events on the Web site to learn more about what might be forthcoming.

Rose aficionados will surely want to include Heirloom Old Garden Roses in their itinerary (see the gardenwalk entry). Located in nearby St. Paul, this Willamette Valley establishment boasts extensive display gardens and is open year-round. You'll see fetching fanfares of old roses, scrumptious modern varieties such as David Austin's English roses, and a 100-foot-long pergola supporting fifty kinds of ramblers.

❀ **Rates:** $$.

Open: Year-round.

Facilities: Four rooms feature queen beds; three suites feature king beds. A wood-burning fireplace and a Jacuzzi highlight the Martini suite. Each room offers a lovely vineyard view; all have private en suite baths. A full breakfast is served daily.

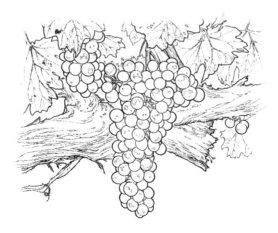

Directions: Youngberg Hill Vineyards is about 40 miles southwest of Portland, approximately an hour's drive. Take I–5 to exit 294 (Highway 99 West, Tigart/Newberg). Travel south on Highway 99W through McMinnville, turning right onto Old Sheridan Highway, then turn right again onto Peavine Road. At Youngberg Hill Road turn left and proceed to the inn. Look on the Web site for detailed directions and a map.

The Lion and the Rose

1810 Northeast Fifteenth Avenue, **Portland,** OR 97212;
(503) 287–9245, (800) 955–1647; www.lionrose.com

LOCATED IN the city's popular Irvington District, the Lion and the Rose is deservedly touted as one of the best bed-and-breakfast inns in Portland. Ensconced in a fine Queen Anne–style home constructed in 1906, the designated landmark building sets the standard for classic Victorian décor.

Enjoy the inn's picturesque rose garden, which beautifies the front yard. Looking out from the rear deck or from the lovely gazebo, you'll see a garden set off by perennial borders, redbrick walkways, and roses, all amid the inn's generous greenery. Seasonal displays of bedding annuals add quite a full, colorful look.

Stroll the surrounding grounds and enjoy the fountains and statuary prominently placed about the lawn on paved islands. These elements, along with specimen trees such as Japanese maples, add opulent touches to the garden design.

At the Lion and the Rose, a series of salon afternoons and evenings frequently take place in spring, summer, and fall. These events combine art exhibitions (with the artist present), wine tasting, entertainment, and delicious food, resulting in a variety of experiences.

❀ **Rates:** $–$$.
Open: Year-round.
Facilities: Six rooms with private baths; one room features a Jacuzzi; each room has unique decor. A full breakfast is served.

Directions: The inn is located on the corner of Northeast Fifteenth Avenue and Schuyler. Take the Rose Quarter exit (exit 302A) off I–5 and turn onto Weidler, then continue east to Northeast Fifteenth Avenue. Go left onto Northeast Fifteenth, continue straight across Broadway, and proceed 1 block to the Lion and the Rose. Detailed directions are found on the Web site.

Terwilliger Vista Bed & Breakfast

515 Southwest Westwood Drive, **Portland,** OR 97201;
(503) 244–0602, (888) 244–0602; www.terwilligervista.com

TERWILLIGER VISTA B&B offers the peace and quiet of a residential area in close proximity to Portland's bustling downtown. Wonderfully situated in the West Hills area of Portland, the half-acre grounds include ivy-covered granite block walls and a lovely terraced lawn and gardens featuring azaleas, camellias, rhododendrons, and fruit trees.

Along one side of the spacious Georgian colonial built in 1941, a superb tulip tree stands sentry. On the front lawn the lush cascading form of a camperdown elm is glorious when leafed out, yet it is arguably even more hauntingly lovely in winter, when its leaves are shed to reveal a network of graceful weeping branches. When the tree's magnificent trunk is exposed, a covering of mosses and lichens imparts an ancient quality to the rare specimen.

Also exceptional in winter are views from Terwilliger Vista's windows. Through a host of deciduous trees one can gaze on the Willamette River, the city's twinkling lights, and Mount Hood's impressive peak, which can be observed changing shape and color as the sky lightens and day breaks.

Just a short walk from the B&B, the Chart House restaurant offers majestic views together with menu specialties such as prime rib and seafood.

❁ **Rates:** $–$$.
Open: Year-round.

Facilities: Three rooms and two suites, all with private baths. The Garden Retreat is graced by a fireplace and queen canopy bed; the expansive Burgundy Rose Suite boasts windows that look out over the Willamette Valley. The Peach Room offers a bay window and views of the rear gardens, while the Green Room and Blue Room each feature a queen bed and cozy furnishings. Common areas include a library and outdoor patios. A full breakfast is served.

Directions: Terwilliger is in Portland's West Hills neighborhood. From I–5 take the Terwilliger Boulevard exit (exit 297) onto Barbur Boulevard, then turn left onto Southwest Terwilliger Boulevard. Go slightly to the right in order to stay on Southwest Terwilliger Boulevard, making a sharp left onto Southwest Westwood Drive. You'll find detailed directions on the Web site.

McMenamins Edgefield

2126 Southwest Halsey, **Troutdale,** OR 97060;
(503) 669–8610, (800) 669–8610; www.mcmenamins.com

ORIGINALLY BUILT in 1911 as the Multnomah County Poor Farm, McMenamins Edgefield is now on the National Register of Historic Places. You can expect to find a good deal more than a place to stay at Edgefield, where hotel guests and visitors enjoy a vineyard and winery, brewery and bar, restaurant, golf course, live music, theater, and more.

The golf course features an unusual design based upon a Scottish-style links course traditionally located by the sea. At Edgefield the greens are maintained while the remaining terrain is natural, with paths mowed through the wild areas so that people can pass through.

Overall, the atmosphere at the thirty-eight-acre estate is lively, with original artwork liberally decorating walls and ceilings, fuse boxes, pipes, and staircases. The landscape boasts a compelling "garden in progress," which covers a third of the property. Garden lovers mark their calendars when McMenamins Edgefield hosts plant sales and occasional gardening seminars, where the ongoing implementation of the estate's lavish plantings is investigated. Seminar themes include "Attracting Butterflies to Your Garden with Native Plants" and "Home Is Where the Habitat Is."

Another popular event attended by green thumbs is the two-day Cracked Pots Garden Artwork Festival, held in summer. Based in Portland, the Cracked Pots group of artists creates unqualifiedly unique objects, functional and decorative, mainly from recycled materials.

Rather than giving the appearance of a commercial enterprise, the Edgefield setting conveys a warm, friendly atmosphere. Here you'll find lush orchards, herb and container gardens, deep flower beds, and bounteous borders featuring unusual annuals and perennials. Head groundskeeper Kim Kincaid mentions other features, such as a beguiling meadow garlanded with perennials and measuring in the vicinity of 10 by 130 feet. And a quarter-acre vegetable production garden supplies the Edgefield kitchen with temperate fruits and seasonal produce.

Kim describes the Edgefield garden style as "informally formal." Visitors have been heard proclaiming it a "gardener's garden." Look for a most unusual garden installation behind the Power Station Pub. At the time the golf course was built, three huge concrete cow-feeding troughs were discovered. Now functioning as a traditional English trough garden, the horticultural display makes a statement with arrays of alpine and rock garden plants.

Visit the Edgefield gardens for yourself, and plan to enjoy Northwest cuisine in the Black Rabbit Restaurant or a casual meal at the Lodging Dock Grill, perhaps sampling one of the fine beers or ales associated with the McMenamins name.

Garden clubs or interested individuals should contact Kim Kincaid in advance to preschedule a tour of the gardens.

❀ **Rates:** $.
Open: Year-round.

Facilities: Sixteen suites with private baths; ninety-eight rooms are designed as European-style lodgings, with centrally located shared baths for men or women. Each shared bath offers a sink, toilet, and shower with total privacy. There are single occupancy rooms, queen and king accommodations featuring sitting rooms, and family rooms sleeping up to six people. The inn also includes hostel accommodations.

Directions: McMenamins Edgefield is about 20 minutes directly east of downtown Portland and about fifteen minutes from the west entrance of the Columbia River Gorge. Take Interstate 84 to exit 16, continuing on 238th Drive south to the first traffic light. Turn left onto Halsey Street, driving east to McMenamins Edgefield. A map, along with public transit and driving directions, are found on the Web site.

Resources for Gardeners

*L*isted under this heading you will find distinctive services and products such as uncommon garden ornaments and some additional Internet sites that post up-to-the-minute events. Rare gardening books, aged chicken manure for your roses, and the perfect cultivating tool can be found here.

There are hundreds of fine plant nurseries and garden centers and other laudable establishments I came across in my travels; however, I could not include them all in this chapter or this book. Don't let that stop you from going farther afield. Allow yourself to wander and you're certain to find additional sites that will stir your particular garden passions.

PERIODICALS AND WEB SITES

The Garden Conservancy's Open Days Directory

P.O. Box 219, **Cold Spring**, NY 10516; (888) 842–2442;
www.gardenconservancy.org

THE GARDEN CONSERVANCY is a national organization that works
to preserve outstanding American gardens and to generate interest
in the country's gardening heritage. Ruth Bancroft's wonderful garden in Northern California is credited with inspiring Frank Cabot
to found the Garden Conservancy. In so doing, Cabot spearheaded
and inspired others to go forward and create a thriving membership,
one that continues to grow and to provide support for gardens from
coast to coast.

Akin to England's National Gardens Scheme, the Garden Conservancy's Open Days Program provides the rare opportunity to visit
private gardens. Like the *Yellow Book* produced by the National
Gardens Scheme, with its listings of gardens that open for charity,
the Garden Conservancy publishes its yearly *Open Days Directory:
The Guide to Visiting America's Best Private Gardens*.

Obtain a copy of the directory to be privy to a schedule of days
when you can enjoy self-guided tours of private sanctuaries you
might never see under any other circumstance—public gardens are
included, too.

If you plan to visit gardens around the country, you may want
to purchase the national edition, with listings for nearly two dozen
states. Have the regional West edition in hand if you are interested
in coordinating visits to gardens while traveling in Washington or
Oregon; the West edition covers the six western states. Other editions include the Northeast, Midwest, and South.

The national edition can be purchased at bookstores or by visiting www.gardenconservancy.org. Regional editions are available
from bookstores, nurseries, or the Garden Conservancy Web site,

where you'll also find prices for the various editions, shipping fees, and discount coupons.

Open dates and times vary from year to year, but gardens must pass muster to be included in the program. Be assured that each special landscape will encompass a worthy garden design and inspirational plantings. Gorgeous views are oftentimes an added bonus.

To plan your itinerary, first peruse the directory to glean a listing of open days by date. You'll find chronological listings by county, then by town. The special days that are set aside unfold from spring through fall, with the names of each garden and a description provided to help you make your selections. A nominal fee is collected at each garden when you visit; no reservations are required. You'll find detailed driving directions included in each garden listing. One free admission coupon is included in each book.

Many garden owners open their gates to the public only once, so in any given year, you may have occasion to experience a glorious and surprising gardenscape that will remain hidden to the public ever after.

Pacific Horticulture magazine

P.O. Box 680, **Berkeley,** CA 94701; (510) 849–1627; www.pacifichorticulture.org

A MATCHLESS RESOURCE for the West Coast's garden and plant lovers, *Pacific Horticulture* magazine offers quarterly issues filled with intelligent writing and exquisite photography. Serious gardeners from Vancouver to San Diego can turn to this periodical for stimulating articles on plants, places, and prominent people that inhabit the realms of gardening, horticulture, and botany. *Pacific Horticulture* also updates readers with book reviews, a "Laboratory Report," and calendar listing of events and happenings throughout California and the Northwest.

Count on *Pacific Horticulture* for its dependably incisive and appealing stories. In one issue, editor Richard G. Turner Jr. set a thoughtful tone with insightful musings on the critique of landscape design. Articles included: "Trees of Golden Gate Park: Silk Oak and Two Lindens," by Elizabeth McClintock; "Coleus," by Richard W. Hartlage; an ode to seasonal highlights at Matanzas Creek Winery gardens, by Julie Greenberg; and an article on Italy's Landriana Gardens, by Joan Tesei.

Pacific Horticulture is published by the nonprofit Pacific Horticultural Foundation, which is supported by the California Horticultural Society, the San Francisco Botanical Garden Society, the Western Horticultural Society, the Southern California Horticultural Society, and the Northwest Horticultural Society. Issues appear quarterly in January, April, July, and October.

Northwest Gardening Connection Web Site

http://dnr.metrokc.gov/wlr/dss/gardening/

CHECK OUT THE Northwest Gardening Connection Web site before visiting the Seattle area and sign up for the mailing list. Once you begin receiving the electronic digest put together by Luanne Coachman for the King County Water and Land Resources Division, you'll have a direct pipeline to all the latest gardening news and happenings throughout King County and beyond.

Click on Gardening Resources and you'll find extensive links to a host of local gardens and nurseries, books, plant societies, natural yard care, and much more. The Event Calendar will help you plan a visit to coincide with a stimulating lecture by a guest speaker on topics ranging from the newest plant introductions to garden travel. Or you might like to attend a meeting of the NW Gardening Connection and enjoy a chance to hobnob with like-minded plant enthusiasts.

Even when I do not expect to be traveling to the Pacific Northwest, I find Luanne's excellent newsletter featuring articles and announcements equally fascinating to peruse from my home in Northern California.

SERVICES, GARDEN SHOPS, AND BOOKSTORES

Victorian Garden Tours

Victoria, BC; (250) 380–2797; www.victoriangardentours.com

ENTHUSIASTIC and eminently knowledgeable, Joan Looy offers customized, interpretive tours of private gardens and public landscapes in Victoria, British Columbia, and its environs. On a tour with Joan or an associate, you'll gain access to gardenscapes that reflect Pacific Northwest style, viewing deeply layered designs created and maintained by homeowners who are avid plant collectors and true colorists.

The enterprise offers guided tours year-round, adjusting to the age and health issues of garden sojourners with an emphasis on accessibility and pacing. Joan shares information on transportation connections to Vancouver Island, and she can also arrange a delightful tea in such magical settings as the Abkhazi Garden tearoom.

Visit the Web site to see examples of tours highlighting seasonal color and other themes. Check out the Garden Gallery, where you can begin to explore the beauty of Victoria and exceptional island settings. Phone for information or e-mail joan@victoriangarden tours.com.

Flora & Fauna Books

121 First Avenue South, Seattle, WA 98104; (206) 623–4727, (206) 623–2001(fax); www.ffbooks.net

BOTANY, HORTICULTURE, ornithology, and all fields of natural history are specialties at David Hutchinson's Flora & Fauna Books, a fascinating bookshop with a most appealing ambience. The stock includes new, out-of-print, rare, and antique books from all over the world.

Flora & Fauna is the sort of shop that invites serious browsing and one that can offer helpful advice to both experts and beginners. Business can be done by mail order, phone, or fax, and you can meet the books and staff at various horticultural and related shows around the country.

Do visit if you are traveling in the Seattle area. Or check the Web site to browse for books online.

❀ **Directions:** The store is located in downtown Seattle, in historic Pioneer Square. See the Web site for detailed directions.

Herban Pottery & Patio

3200 First Avenue South, **Seattle,** WA 98134; (206) 749-5112, (800) 618-4742; www.herbanpottery.com

HERBAN POTTERY carries a cornucopia of terra-cotta vessels, garden ornaments, and patio furniture from around the world. Classically styled Italian urns, colorful one-of-a-kind hand-painted pots, decorative birdbaths, and handsome benches were some of the treasures I found when I perused the wares at this lively Seattle store.

Herban Pottery's diverse inventory intermingles elegant Renaissance forms with casual south-of-the-border motifs. Flower boxes, hanging planters, jumbo Tuscan olive jars, and pottery of every shape, size, and design are displayed. I could easily envision colorful annuals spilling over the robust rim of a lovely Barcelona basketweave pot.

Whether you tend a low-maintenance patio, pamper a backyard cottage garden, or care for a rural woodland retreat, plan a shopping expedition here and you'll find delightful garden accoutrements, fountains, and a wealth of patio furniture—more than a dozen manufacturers are represented.

Other Great Resources

Great resources are scattered throughout this book. Here are a few you don't want to miss:

BC Ferries provides service to nearly fifty ports of call along the coast of British Columbia, and its Web site at www.bcferries.com offers maps of ferry routes, schedules, and some terrific trip-planning aids. See page 44.

The Land Conservancy (TLC) is a nonprofit organization that works to preserve plant habitats and safeguard scenic sites throughout British Columbia. Its Web site (www.conservancy .bc.ca) will guide you to noteworthy conservation projects and great gardening events. See page 49.

Victoria Clipper departs from Pier 69 in Seattle and offers easy access to Vancouver Island and points beyond. Call (800) 888–2535 to receive a Clipper Vacations booklet. See page 84.

Seattle's Northwest Flower & Garden Show (www.gardenshow .com) presents five acres of tantalizing garden exhibits each February in what is the Northwest's top-notch exhibition of all things green and growing. See page 88.

The Bainbridge in Bloom Garden Tour, held each July by the Bainbridge Island Arts and Humanities Council, takes you to five sophisticated gardens and offers lectures, plant sales, and more. Visit www.gardentour.info or read more on page 106.

The Sequim Lavender Festival is a delightful celebration of everything lavender on the third weekend of each July on Washington's North Olympic Peninsula. Log on to www.lavenderfestival.com or see page 114.

The Hardy Plant Society of Oregon (HPSO) focuses on the Pacific Northwest. It offers a stimulating newsletter, great educational programs, and a user-friendly, information-rich Web site (www.hardyplantsociety.org). See page 163.

❄ **Directions:** Located in the SODO (south-of-downtown) neighborhood, 1 mile south of Safeco Field; call for detailed driving directions. Open Tuesday through Saturday 10:00 A.M. to 6:00 P.M., Sunday 11:00 A.M. to 5:00 P.M.; call to confirm hours.

Lucca Statuary—European Garden Ornaments Ltd.

3623 Leary Way NW, Seattle, WA 98107; (206) 789–8444; www.luccastatuary.com

LUCCA STATUARY encompasses a vast display space filled with unique cast stone and concrete pieces.

Among the treasure trove of Italian and English–inspired garden ornaments—which overflow the establishment's indoor showrooms and outdoor patio areas—is a lavish presentation of planters and urns, benches and fountains, birdbaths, pedestals, and statues for every sort of garden environment.

Bringing together an extensive collection of pieces with a range of appealing finishes, Lucca Statuary offers sensational possibilities for a variety of stylistic sensibilities. I found myself responding to pots displaying raised acanthus motifs and to the Montecarlo urn, with its fluid, curvilinear design. The classical lines of the Roma urn or Vaso Paladino planter would befit any elegant garden setting. A formal landscape would be enhanced by the Della Robbia wall fountain or Spanish lion pond.

If you're thinking of adding something special to your garden at home, plan a brief detour from your itinerary of gardenwalks to visit Seattle's Lucca Statuary. Be prepared to spend time pondering over the shop's huge selection of adornments.

❄ **Directions:** Located west of Highway 99 at Northwest Thirty-ninth Street and Leary Way NW. Look for a map on the Web site, where you can also preview the store's interior and alluring merchandise. Open seven days a week; call for seasonal hours.

Powell's Books for Cooks & Gardeners

3747 Southeast Hawthorne Boulevard, **Portland,** OR 97214;
(800) 878–7323; www.powells.com

POWELL'S ENORMOUS "City of Books" store at 1005 West Burnside Street in Portland is a book lover's paradise. One of the nation's great bookstores (perhaps the largest), Powell's main store occupies an entire city block.

With six stores in Portland and a total of five warehouses, Powell's operates a specialty store with gardeners in mind: Books for Cooks & Gardeners features a fine selection of rare and collectible volumes for those of us with a penchant for the beauty of aged illustrations, fragile vellum, or flowery prose.

You'll also want to pore over the store's gardening remainders and sale books. I love to browse through reprints of early gardening literature, finding it fascinating to ruminate on the concerns voiced by garden writers of years gone by.

Depending on when you travel to Portland, you might like to attend a special event. Check the Web site to see if any appearances by gardening authors are scheduled.

If gardening books are not temptation enough, an array of garden ornaments and other essentials are enticingly displayed, from handsome pottery, planters, and birdbaths to herbal hand creams, gardening gloves, and the like.

❀ **Directions:** The store is located in Portland's trendy Hawthorne neighborhood. Visit the Web site to see a map or call for driving directions. Monday through Saturday 9:00 A.M. to 9:00 P.M., and Sunday 9:00 A.M. to 8:00 P.M.; closed Thanksgiving.

Smith & Hawken stores

www.smithandhawken.com

WASHINGTON
Bellevue: 12200 Northup Way; (425) 881–6775
Seattle: Northeast University Village;
4622 Twenty-fifth Avenue NE; (206) 985–8613

OREGON
Portland: 26 Northwest Twenty-third Place; (503) 274–9561

NO OTHER ENTERPRISE equals the high visibility and panache associated with Smith & Hawken's ever-expanding line of accoutrements—from useful, well-made tools for maintaining a garden to
aesthetic embellishments that tickle one's fancy.

With its classic garden furnishings and comfortably cosmopol-
itan apparel, Smith & Hawken has been at the forefront of the gardening blitz that's sweeping the country. Whether you wish to create
a personal garden sanctuary outdoors or introduce a decorative
botanical theme indoors, you'll find a wealth of furnishings and
accessories at Smith & Hawken.

There are a slew of shops on the West Coast, so if you find yourself in the neighborhood of a Smith & Hawken store, pay a visit and
see if you can resist *not* buying something for yourself or a special
friend who gardens.

❀ **Directions:** Call individual Smith & Hawken stores for hours and directions. Detailed driving directions are also posted on the Web site.

Choosing an Outing

ARBORETUMS AND CONSERVATION SITES

British Columbia
The Horticulture Centre
Queen Elizabeth Park

Washington
Meerkerk Rhododendron
  Gardens
Sehome Hill Arboretum
Washington Park Arboretum

Oregon
Washington Park's Hoyt
  Arboretum

ARTISTIC GARDENS

British Columbia
Arthur Erickson House and
  Garden
Southlands Nursery Ltd.

Washington
Little and Lewis Garden Gallery

Oregon
Dancing Oaks Nursery
Hogan and Sanderson Garden

BONSAI GARDENS

Washington
Pacific Rim Bonsai Collection

BOTANICAL GARDENS AND CONSERVATORIES

British Columbia
Bloedel Floral Conservatory at
  Queen Elizabeth Park
University of British Columbia
  Botanical Garden
VanDusen Botanical Garden

Washington
Bellevue Botanical Garden
Medicinal Herb Garden,
 University of Washington
Meerkerk Rhododendron Gardens
Rhododendron Species
 Foundation and Botanical
 Garden
Volunteer Park Conservatory
W. W. Seymour Botanical
 Conservatory at Wright Park

Oregon
The Berry Botanic Garden
Crystal Springs Rhododendron
 Garden
Leach Botanical Garden

CHILD-PLEASING GARDENS

British Columbia
Bloedel Floral Conservatory at
 Queen Elizabeth Park
Minter Country Garden Centre
Minter Gardens
Stanley Park
VanDusen Botanical Garden
Victoria Butterfly Gardens

Washington
Fragrance Garden at Tennant Lake
 Interpretive Center and
 Hovander Homestead Park
Peace Arch State Park

Oregon
Ira C. Keller Memorial Fountain
 Park
The Oregon Garden

CHINESE GARDENS

British Columbia
Dr. Sun Yat-Sen Classical
 Chinese Garden

Washington
Seattle Chinese Garden
 (Xi Hua Yuan) at South Seattle
 Community College

Oregon
Portland Classical Chinese Garden

CLASSIC NORTHWEST AND HERITAGE GARDENS

British Columbia
Abkhazi Garden
The Butchart Gardens
Milner Gardens and Woodland

Washington
The Bloedel Reserve
The Chase Garden
Dunn Gardens
Heronswood Nursery Ltd.
Lakewold Gardens
PowellsWood—
 A Northwest Garden

Oregon
Connie Hansen Garden
Elk Rock, the Garden at the
 Bishop's Close
The Grotto

CONTEMPORARY, MODERNIST GARDENS

British Columbia
Arthur Erickson House
 and Garden

HISTORIC GARDENS

British Columbia
Government House Gardens

Washington
Hovander Homestead Park

Oregon
Elk Rock, the Garden at the
   Bishop's Close
The Grotto
Historic Deepwood Estate Gardens
Shore Acres State Park Garden

JAPANESE GARDENS

British Columbia
Nitobe Memorial Garden

Washington
Kubota Garden
Washington Park Arboretum's
   Japanese Garden

Oregon
Washington Park's Japanese
   Garden

PARKS AND PUBLIC SPACES

British Columbia
Beacon Hill Park
Government House Gardens
Queen Elizabeth Park
Stanley Park
Victoria's Hanging Baskets

Washington
Bainbridge Public Library Gardens
Bradner Gardens Park
Fragrance Garden at Tennant Lake
   Interpretive Center and
   Hovander Homestead Park
Parsons Garden
Peace Arch State Park
Point Defiance Park Gardens
Volunteer Park

Oregon
Bush's Pasture Park
Hendricks Park Rhododendron
   Garden

Ira C. Keller Memorial
   Fountain Park
Kaiser Permanente's Tualatin
   Poison Prevention Garden
Shore Acres State Park Garden
Washington Park

ROSE GARDENS

British Columbia
The Butchart Gardens

Washington
Point Defiance Park Gardens
Woodland Park Rose Garden

Oregon
Bush's Pasture Park
Heirloom Roses
Owen Memorial Rose Garden
Peninsula Park Rose Garden
Shore Acres State Park Garden
Washington Park's International
   Rose Test Garden

SHOW GARDENS

British Columbia
The Butchart Gardens
Minter Gardens
Victoria Butterfly Gardens

Oregon
The Oregon Garden

SPECIALTY PLANT NURSERIES AND DISPLAY GARDENS

British Columbia
Minter Country Garden Centre
Southlands Nursery Ltd.

Washington
Cedarbrook Herb Farm

Cultus Bay Nursery & Garden
Heronswood Nursery Ltd.
Hummingbird Farm Nursery and
    Gardens
Molbak's Nursery

Oregon
Adelman Peony Gardens
Cistus Nursery

Cooley's Gardens
Dancing Oaks Nursery
Gossler Farms Nursery
Greer Gardens
Heirloom Roses
Joy Creek Nursery
Nichols Garden Nursery
Siskiyou Rare Plant Nursery

Glossary

allée: A formal element in garden design, such as a long pathway, connecting road, or avenue running between queues of symmetrically planted trees.

arbor: A structure that may serve as an entryway or focal point within the garden, often providing support for climbing vines or roses.

arboretum: A site dedicated to the cultivation and study of trees.

bog: A consistently wet garden area; a habitat specifically designed to remain waterlogged in order to grow plants known to thrive in damp conditions.

bonsai: An art form encompassing venerated techniques for growing dwarf trees or shrubs in ornamental shapes; also refers to a plant pruned and trained in this way.

bromeliad: A large family of primarily tropical plants, many of which grow on trees or rocks in natural settings and derive moisture and nutritional sustenance from the air. Some types of bromeliads grow in terrestrial environments where porous plant matter accumulates, such as the forest floor.

copse: A gathering or small grove of trees or shrubs.

Craftsman style: Spanning the years 1876 to 1916, this architectural style was inspired by nature and craft traditions. The Craftsman bungalow appears to hug the earth, with a distinctly horizontal design: Interiors exhibit a rather open floor plan. Use of local materials is common, such as stone for fireplaces, decorative wrought iron, and simple but abundant woodwork—ceiling beams, built-in shelves, wainscoting, and the like.

cycad: Primitive, cone-bearing evergreen plants; palm or fernlike in appearance.

epiphyte: A type of plant that grows on another plant for support but not for its nutrients; examples include nonparasitic plants such as certain orchids. Also known as an air plant because it does not grow in soil.

espalier: A method whereby fruit trees, roses, etc., are trained to grow on a single, planar surface, such as a building wall or a fence, using wires to support particular branches; designs vary from elaborate crisscross patterns to a layout of horizontal or vertical lines.

garden room: A separate, enclosed area within a larger garden, designed to celebrate a unique idea or character. Room boundaries may be created with hedges, walls of brick or stone, or changes in elevation.

gazebo: A pavilion-like structure placed for viewing the garden. Early examples were traditionally designed as six-sided buildings, commonly incorporating filigree metalwork as decorative embellishment. Contemporary gazebos often feature airy designs of open latticework.

hardscaping: Refers to hard materials used in a garden plan, adding definition and substance to the landscaping. Examples include decorative garden structures such as arbors, paved brick paths, ornamental fences, stone walls, rock work encircling ponds, and wooden frames surrounding raised beds.

herbaceous: Nonwoody plants differentiated by top growth that generally dies back to the ground in winter.

Italianate gardens: A style inspired by Italian architecture and garden design. It may incorporate elaborate roofing tiles, intricate stonework, classical statuary, lavish urns, or formal plantings of shrubbery clipped into geometric shapes, archways, or windowlike openings framing a particular vista.

knot garden: Herbs and/or low hedges such as box planted in a decorative knot design. This garden style dates to the sixteenth century.

mesic: A habitat characterized by regular amounts of moisture.

orangery: Citrus trees cultivated in a greenhouse setting, or orange trees planted outdoors in a decorative manner, as in a courtyard where the trees are arranged according to a particular design.

outcropping: A rocky formation that supports alpine types of plants. In a garden setting, it may allude to a rock of outstanding shape or color set in place to achieve a natural appearance.

parterre: Garden beds shaped in pleasing configurations. They may be outlined by shrubs such as boxwood and feature ornamental flowers or herbs planted within.

pergola: A garden structure much like an elongated arbor, with vertical posts and a horizontal framework or latticework overhead to support climbing plants.

peristyle: A type of courtyard surrounded (or enclosed) by columns; an arrangement of evenly spaced columns encircling a building.

pollard: The technique of severely cutting back the branches of a tree to its trunk either to restrict growth, to promote dense foliage or, more traditionally, to produce straight new shoots for garden use such as stakes.

rill: A formal water feature, often constructed in concrete or stone: A rill is generally designed as a straight, narrow channel that moves water from one level or terrace to the next. A rill's function as an element of garden design is to direct the eyes up or down a slope or across an expanse.

riparian: Along the banks of a river or other watercourse.

scree: A garden habitat that has been implemented with a combination of rocks, gravel, and sand to simulate the type of drainage and overall growing conditions found in natural settings where alpine plants thrive; an accumulation of rock and rubble found on a slope or at the base of a mountain.

secret garden: A secluded area within the overall plan of a garden meant to please and surprise visitors and to function as an intimate retreat.

tableau: A conspicuous garden scene where plants and design components come together to produce an especially delightful scene.

vignette: The successful combination of various garden elements into a unified point of interest or tableau. It may include alluring plant associations and attractive garden structures or take in a picturesque view.

Index of Gardens